NEW PERSPECTIVES IN SOCIOLOGY

Edited by John Wakeford

This series provides an opportunity for young sociologists
to present original material and also to summarise and
review critically certain key themes and controversies
in their subject. All the authors are experts in their own
field and each monograph not only provides in an
accessible form stimulating ideas for the specialist but
also represents in itself a significant personal contribution
to the discipline.

Students of sociology will find the series invaluable. For
non-specialists the monographs provide a clear and
authoritative insight into the concerns and perspectives
of the modern sociologist.

Other titles in the Series

Social Research
in
Bethnal Green

An evaluation of the work of the Institute of Community Studies

JENNIFER PLATT

Lecturer in Sociology, University of Sussex

MACMILLAN

First published 1971 by
MACMILLAN AND CO LTD
London and Basingstoke
Associated companies in New York Toronto
Dublin Melbourne Johannesburg and Madras

SBN 333 10088 3 (hard cover)
333 10092 1 (paper cover)

Printed in Great Britain by
ROBERT MACLEHOSE AND CO LTD
The University Press, Glasgow

e²

For My Parents

Contents

Preface

The first idea of this book arose in discussion at Macmillans of where the gaps lay in sociology that a publisher could usefully attempt to fill. It was felt then that textbooks were common enough, and monographs arose naturally from research interest, but that there were very few examples of the intermediate genre that reviews a body of existing research at a level such that it may be of use to students, and yet interest those who are already professionals in the field. This book aims to help fill that gap.

The Institute of Community Studies, and Peter Willmott in particular, have been most helpful in the preparation of the Introduction and Bibliography, checking the accuracy of historical and bibliographical detail, giving me offprints, and providing unpublished information about various aspects of the Institute's work and plans. I would like to thank them very warmly for all their help, and hope that they will not feel that this is too ungrateful a return.

I would also like to thank a number of colleagues for their useful comments on drafts: Geoff Ingham on the whole, David Oldman on the two chapters on research methods, Aaron Sloman on the chapter 'Value Judgements and Policy Recommendations'. Many points have also profited from comments made by students in discussion of the books. Finally, my thanks to my husband, Charles Goldie, for his moral support and for playing the role of stylistic critic and interested layman.

University of Sussex   Jennifer Platt
December 1969

1 Introduction

The Institute of Community Studies is a phenomenon. It started on a modest scale in 1954, and in the fifteen years since then has produced a continuous flow of books and papers and policy suggestions; its work has become probably more widely known in Britain than that of any other social research institute, though judgements of its value have varied considerably. Some of its books seem to have influenced the whole outlook of many young people, and I suspect that the general reading public's conception of sociology is based largely on this body of work; academic sociologists, however, have often not been happy to accept this identification. It seems an appropriate time at which to attempt a full-scale evaluation of the work of what is by now an established institution, and to see if the conflicting opinions held of it can be reconciled, or if they rest on divergent standards and interests.

The Institute's broad policy, as described on the dust jacket of each of its books, is as follows:

> In approach, the Institute had tried to bring some of the strengths of anthropology to sociology, combining personal observations and illustration with statistical analysis. The aim is to undertake research which will both add to basic knowledge about society and illuminate practical questions of social policy, and to publish the findings in a form which will interest the layman as well as the specialist.

The original purpose has been stated more precisely in an article as being

> ... to study the relationship between the social services and working-class family life. The assumption was that the

1

policy-makers and administrators were (to use a somewhat elusive term) *insufficiently* aware of the needs or views of the working-class people who form the bulk of the users of social services, and we hoped that social research might help to provide a more realistic basis for policy . . . we had, as well as the desire to derive practical suggestions about policy, some broader interests. We wanted to find out more about the structure and functioning of the family in industrial society, and about working-class patterns of life. We hoped too that our investigations would throw light upon some current social trends. . . .[1] *

These ideas have been modified and developed somewhat in the course of the Institute's history, but in broad outline they have been consistently followed. Thus the commitment in terms of subject matter has been to a concern with the relationship of working-class people to the social services, and the ways in which these services can be improved to meet the felt needs of their consumers; the commitment in terms of method has been to a combination of personal involvement in case studies and of generalisation from statistically adequate samples. Linking these two themes has been the determination to make the research results accessible to the layman, so that the chances of practical influence on public policy at all levels are increased.

The Institute started in 1954 with two research projects in Bethnal Green.† The first, published as 'Family and Kinship in East London', was initially concerned with the effect on the family of moving from Bethnal Green to a new housing estate, 'Greenleigh'. In the early stages of their research, however, Michael Young and Peter Willmott found that wider family relationships were so important to their respondents that the project became equally a study of the nature of the extended family in Bethnal Green. Some aspects of the kinship system there were attributed by the researchers to

* Throughout this book purely bibliographical notes are numbered and placed at pp. 144-50, while substantive ones that add to the text are asterisked and placed at the foot of the page.

† A complete list of the Institute's publications, in chronological order, will be found in the Bibliography. In this brief account the publications arising out of each research project will be referred to in parentheses by the numbers they are given in the Bibliography.

2

the fact that it was a homogeneously working-class area; therefore a comparative study was undertaken in a middle-class area to explore these ideas further (4). Greenleigh had been studied when it had only been in existence for a few years, and clearly some of the then apparent consequences of rehousing might have been chiefly due to novelty; thus this led on to a study by Peter Willmott of the long-established L.C.C. housing estate at Dagenham (8). Peter Marris again studied the effects of a public rehousing scheme on an established community, although in a very different setting, when he investigated a slum clearance programme in Lagos (5). These continuing interests in housing policy and planning were also expressed in a number of smaller studies of a more limited nature, often undertaken in conjunction with architects or planners and published in their journals (26, 33, 39, 40, 41, 42, 45, 47).

The second of the initial projects in Bethnal Green was Peter Townsend's work on old people; he set out to investigate how far they were isolated from their families, and to discuss the implications for their needs from the social services (2). This has been followed by other studies, again in Bethnal Green, of special groups and their problems. Peter Marris studied the problems created by widowhood, and its social and emotional impact on young widows (3); Enid Mills investigated the family's role in relation to mental patients, and the consequences of their illnesses for the family (6). In slightly different vein, since teenage boys could not in the same sense be regarded as a group with problems, Peter Willmott has filled out the picture of family life in Bethnal Green further by exploration of their position and role, and more specifically of their educational attitudes and involvement in delinquent behaviour (13).

Several of these books are concerned in one way or another with the social services, and this original interest eventually led to intensive study of medical services in the country as a whole. Ann Cartwright used a national sample to find out about patients' experiences in hospitals (9); in 1963 the Institute set up a distinct Medical Care Research Unit under her direction, and this has subsequently produced a study of patients' relationships with their general practitioners (15), as well as a number of related pieces of work

3

(43, 51, 52, 53). A yet broader interest in general problems of social policy is shown in Peter Marris and Martin Rein's 'Dilemmas of Social Reform'. This came out of a year spent by Peter Marris in the United States studying the operation and effectiveness of programmes designed to combat the handicaps of poverty, and discusses the political and practical problems involved in alternative strategies of reform.

Another major research area has been in education, and here the studies have been diverse and not very closely related to each other. The first, 'Education and the Working Class', was initiated outside the Institute and based on Huddersfield; it was about the effects on a group of working-class children of going to grammar school. This was followed by another book by one of the authors, Brian Jackson, again rather outside the main line of the Institute's work, on streaming in primary schools (11). Peter Marris contributed to the discussion around the Robbins Report by comparing student social groupings and attitudes at two universities and a college of advanced technology, and drawing some conclusions about the relation between the student's experiences and university ideals (10). Michael Young wrote a general book on the need for action research on detailed educational policy, making the first Institute book not based on a social survey (12); he then followed his own recommendations by conducting an experiment in a primary school, on the effects of an attempt to involve parents more in the school's activities on their children's academic achievement (17).

New projects under way which, at the time of writing, have not yet reached the stage of publication include ones on family planning advice and its sources, on the growth of African entrepreneurship in Kenya, on the use of medicines, on home care for the dying, and on the relationships between work, family life and leisure patterns and their consequences for the physical environment in the London Metropolitan Region.[2] *

Thus it can be seen that the Institute's work has developed in ways that were not fully anticipated in its original

* The remaining book to appear in the Institute's series is W. G. Runciman's 'Relative Deprivation and Social Justice' (Routledge & Kegan Paul, 1966); this was initiated outside the Institute, and is very different in character from all their other books, although without the association it would probably have differed further.

4

purposes, although they are in no way inconsistent with them. In part this has depended on the internal dynamics of the research process itself, with one investigation bringing new problems to light which form the basis of the next; in part it has depended on the personal interests of individuals, and in part on the availability of funds.*

The four main members of the Institute's research staff have been Michael Young, Peter Willmott, Peter Marris and Ann Cartwright; others have been more transient, some of them associated with projects that never reached publication. Peter Townsend is now Professor of Sociology at the University of Essex, and has continued to do his own research on the problems of old age; Dennis Marsden also teaches at the University of Essex; Brian Jackson is Director of the Advisory Centre for Education in Cambridge, and continues to write on educational issues and working-class culture; Enid Mills teaches at Eastbourne College of Education. Of the four main research workers, Peter Willmott has been fairly consistently associated with community research in some way related to Bethnal Green and with housing and planning issues, and Ann Cartwright has always

* The Elmgrant Trust, in giving a grant for research for 'Family and Kinship in East London', made it possible to establish the Institute; it also financed 'Relative Deprivation and Social Justice'. The Nuffield Foundation financed part or all of the research for 'The Family Life of Old People', 'Innovation and Research in Education', 'Adolescent Boys of East London', 'Learning Begins at Home', and other studies in education and town planning; the Nuffield Provincial Hospitals Trust gave support to most of the work on hospitals.

The Joseph Rowntree Memorial Trust financed part or all of the research for 'Family and Class in a London Suburb', 'Education and the Working Class', 'Living with Mental Illness', 'Evolution of a Community', 'Human Relations and Hospital Care', 'The Experience of Higher Education', 'Adolescent Boys of East London', 'Streaming', and several smaller studies. The Ford Foundation financed part or all of the research for 'Family and Kinship in East London', 'Widows and their Families', 'Family and Class in a London Suburb', 'Adolescent Boys of East London', and 'Dilemmas of Social Reform'. The Leverhulme Trust financed part or all of the research for 'Family and Social Change in an African City', 'The Evolution of a Community', and 'The Experience of Higher Education'. In addition to these sources, support has also been received for single projects from the Mental Health Research Fund ('Living with Mental Illness'), the Gulbenkian Foundation ('Innovation and Research in Education'), the U.S. President's Committee on Juvenile Delinquency and Youth Crime ('Dilemmas of Social Reform'), the U.S. Public Health Service ('Patients and their Doctors'), the Department of Education and Science ('Learning Begins at Home'), and the Ministry of Housing and Local Government, the Department of Health and Social Security, the Eugenics Society and the College of General Practitioners for research published in article form or incorporated in other reports.

5

worked on medical subjects; Michael Young has become increasingly involved in educational research, with some work on factors involved in social mobility; Peter Marris has worked on a number of topics, but has shown a special interest in African problems. Three of these four have had continuous careers at the Institute over a long period of time; Michael Young has had many other activities, spending three years teaching at Cambridge and three as Chairman of the Social Science Research Council, to mention only the main ones. The academic backgrounds and training of the research workers have been diverse, and apparently those with formal qualifications in sociology have always been in a minority, although related disciplines such as social anthropology, history and economics have been represented.* Internal training of new members has taken place on the job, and occasional use has been made of outside courses.

The variety of subjects dealt with in the series of publications has meant that many different audiences have been interested in them. All, however, have some claim to fall within the broad general area of sociology, although the authors have made it clear that their primary intended audience has never been one of professional sociologists. Most of the books have been reviewed both in the strictly sociological journals and in the professional journals of those who are responsible for practical applications; many of them have also been brought to the attention of wider publics still by reviews and comments in newspapers and general periodicals. There have been extremely favourable reviews — for example:

> ... the bones of hardwon statistics are astutely given flesh and life by some colourful case-histories and highly quotable opinions. And there is one other outstanding quality in the work of Dr Young and his colleagues: it owes as much to the indigenous tradition of Charles Booth as to 'Middletown', and is suffused with a not wholly disguised humanism which in itself contributes to interested writing

* Michael Young holds a B.Sc. in Economics and a Ph.D. in Social Administration, and is a barrister-at-law; Peter Willmott took an external B.A. in Sociology in 1959; Peter Marris's B.A. was in Philosophy and Psychology; Ann Cartwright's B.A. and Ph.D. are in Statistics, and before joining the Institute she was a Lecturer in Social Medicine at Edinburgh University.

6

and therefore interesting reading. ('Times Literary Supplement', on 'Family and Class in a London Suburb')[3]

I doubt if it could be improved on. It is well written, painstaking, scrupulously fair, and above all open-hearted. (Ian Nairn on 'The Evolution of a Community', in the 'Daily Telegraph')[4]

The study is a model application of sociological acumen to a complex social and economic problem. . . . ('The Economist', on 'Family and Social Change in an African City')[5]

There have also been strong criticisms — not always consistent with each other, as the following extracts show:

The statistical analysis of the data is slight, the evidence is mainly in the form of quotations from interview notes, and the result is a restatement in largely impressionistic form of the sort of thing about neighbouring and social relations with which we are already thoroughly familiar. . . . It is curious that this kind of misleading reportage should have been allowed to pass when Willmott is so well aware of the similar danger involved in the excessive use of statistical apparatus in social research reports. . . . (Maurice Broady on 'The Evolution of a Community', in the 'Sociological Review')[6]

While appreciating the amount of work which has gone into Mr Willmott's study, one cannot help wishing that he had been a little less anxious to substantiate his statements by supplying such a distracting wealth of references. (Audrey Powell on 'The Evolution of a Community', in the 'Sunday Times')[7]

Despite an occasional attempt to document the epidemiological significance of her findings, Mills indicates an awareness of the limitations of the data by wisely eschewing the pursuit of statistical inference . . . the reader is too often subjected to a rash of dramatic portraits that do more to caricature these patients than to offer the

7

insights that were obviously intended . . . . (Mark Lefton on 'Living with Mental Illness', in the 'American Sociological Review')[8]

. . . the book is descriptive and analyses are not related to, nor do they lead to, sociological hypotheses. The book has twelve chapters which do not appear to be ordered with any specific theme in mind. There is no historical perspective. . . . While such works have made a contribution to understanding health services . . . their contribution to the maturation of medical sociology specifically and to sociology in general remains equivocal. (Milton S. Davis on 'Patients and their Doctors', in the 'American Sociological Review')[9]

Although both favourable and unfavourable comments have appeared in all kinds of sources, it is probably true in general to say that where the sociological journals have commented on the manner in which the conclusions were reached, as opposed to the conclusions themselves, the tone has tended to be unfavourable; outside these professional journals the balance has been much more favourable, with more interest taken in the conclusions than the methods, and any criticism has tended to fall on the presence of the tables and statistics of which the professionals thought that there should be more. Strong feelings have been excited in both directions about the general merits of the books.

Despite this professional criticism, academic sociologists have made considerable use of the Institute's findings, particularly those in the earlier books.[10] Further, other studies have been undertaken which relate to their work in various ways. A directly comparative study has been done in Swansea,[11] and other work has been formulated in ways influenced by their findings. Thus the Institute's works have been implicitly included in 'the literature' by sociologists working in relevant fields.

A review of reviews might suggest only the simple conclusion that you can't please everybody, and that the Institute has inevitably laid itself open to many criticisms by setting out to address itself simultaneously to diverse audiences. The rest of this book tries to probe deeper than such a conclusion. Clearly the work of the Institute must be

8

evaluated in terms of its own declared aims, and this will involve considering whether the means adopted have been those best calculated to achieve such aims. One may also, however, legitimately ask whether the aims are realistic ones, and indeed whether, in the light of alternative value systems, they are desirable ones.

The main concern of this book will be to evaluate the Institute's contribution to contemporary sociology; this means that other kinds of contribution, for instance to planning or to social work, will be considered only insofar as the apparent aims of particular works make it necessary. The bases on which judgements are made will be made more explicit as the issues arise. Since we are concerned with the Institute as such, the few books published in its series but written by authors who have not been fully associated with it [12] will be excluded, as will work done in other contexts by the central authors.

2 Value Judgements and Policy Recommendations

It is difficult, but necessary, to write in general terms about the value judgements and policy recommendations made by the Institute of Community Studies. It is necessary because these are so clearly at the centre of the interests and motives of its members; it is difficult because they are not always explicitly stated, and are scattered through numbers of books and articles which may not be entirely consistent with each other. I shall try, therefore, to strike a balance between constructing a stereotype of the views of the Institute as a whole and analysing each book separately in detail. The structure of the chapter will be to consider first the general value judgements made, and then the nature and appropriateness of the policy recommendations that follow from them.

Value Judgements

The Institute's general policy statements[1] make clear the commitment to relevance to social problems, but the only formal indication of a specific standpoint in relation to them is in the expressed concern to take into account the viewpoint of the consumer of social policy, particularly the working-class consumer. This implies an important value judgement, but one whose full consequences cannot be known until the investigation of viewpoints has taken place. It tends to suggest that the consumer is seen as likely to be hostile towards or dissatisfied with current policies, or that there is at least an implicit conflict of interest between consumer and producer.

This general standpoint is exemplified in particular cases by the whole basis on which the research projects have been planned. The projects bearing on housing policy investigate the opinions and behaviour patterns of the people who live in

10

different kinds of housing; the projects on medical care investigate the patients; the projects on widows, old people and the mentally ill investigate the problems of these groups as they themselves perceive and define them. The opinions of these subjects are not always directly elicited, but they are treated as important; the authors of the various books obviously regard their levels of satisfaction as a major criterion for the adequacy of social policy. This may be illustrated by some quotations:

> People should obviously have as much choice of residence as possible: given choice, they will be able to meet best the individual needs of which they, and they only, should be the judge. ('Family and Kinship in East London', pp. 155-6)

> ... good communication has been defined in terms of patients feeling satisfied that they were able to find out what they wanted to know. ('Problems of Hospital Communication', p. 117)

> Even where the parents were agreeable [to home visits from teachers]. . . . A child may want . . . to keep the two halves of his life separate, and to find a refuge in each from the other. ('Learning Begins at Home', p. 123)

As this last quotation shows, the emphasis on the importance of individual preferences is strong enough to extend even to children of primary school age, where it might commonly not be regarded as relevant.

Closely related to this value theme are two others, one of which is concerned with the dignity and respect due to the individual as such, and the other of which takes up again the question of preferences as they are expressed in behaviour rather than formulated opinions. Peter Townsend, in 'The Family Life of Old People', argues that opportunities of special employment for old men no longer capable of competing in the ordinary labour market should be provided simply for the sake of their self-respect and social position within the family (p. 151). Peter Marris suggests that an adequate social insurance scheme should enable widows not merely to subsist but to maintain their former status (p. 102). Enid Mills implies that the dignity and feelings of the mentally ill should be considered, and not only (though perhaps mainly) because this is likely to make them co-operate more willingly in treatment. Michael Young, in 'Innovation and Research in Education', holds that among the objects of educational reform should be ' . . . to treat children as individuals rather than as junior members of a mass society' (p. 134).

On the question of the preferences expressed in behaviour patterns, the most direct statement is in an article by Peter Willmott: 'What is needed is more factual information about which obligations are actually undertaken in British society, so that social administration can be brought into line with customary practice.'[2] This kind of point is made more indirectly by the character of the policy recommendations typically made; they suggest alterations in official policies rather than measures designed to bring about changes in the patterns of consumer behaviour which, in conjunction with existing policies, create problems.

The last diffuse values which we can isolate are of tolerance of diversity, and a dislike for striving or competitiveness. These two coexist in a potentially rather uneasy relationship, since the differentiation which promotes diversity is sometimes associated with striving. (This tension, however, is not expressed.) The high value attached to tolerance of diversity is, of course, shown by the general emphasis on the need for planning to allow scope for individual preferences, but it is also stated more overtly. In 'Family and Class in a London Suburb', for instance, the authors say:

> To get on well, people have to some extent to put on a front of *bonhomie*, and maybe leave out some part of their personality in the process. . . . Maybe uniformity is one of the prices we have to pay for sociability in a more mobile society. (p. 129)

In Peter Willmott's study of Dagenham, he defines as a problem of an almost exclusively working-class community

12

... that those who grow up in it with intellectual or cultural talents or interests, or indeed with other kinds of interests which do not fit into the conventional mould, may lack stimulus or encouragement, or may find the pressures to conformity too inhibiting, their opportunities restricted, their life cramped. (pp. 116-17)

It is in similar contexts, of comparison between middle-class and working-class value systems, that judgements about striving are made, and again we quote:

[In Bethnal Green] ... the network of personal relationships acts as a check on the acquisitiveness of local people ... all classes in Woodford are more and more striving to earn more and spend it on the same things. ... Most people seem contented enough with the result. ('Family and Class in a London Suburb', pp. 130, 132)

... to the outsider, competition between neighbours certainly seems less keen, anxiety over possessions less sharp, at Dagenham than elsewhere. ... There is little sign of status striving. ('The Evolution of a Community', p. 100)

The judgements here are not explicitly formulated as such, but tone and context make the evaluative weight attached to the descriptions clear. A preference is implied for the social atmosphere of the working-class communities, and this preference is obviously linked with or derived from a general egalitarianism.

To this set of very general values we may add some more precise and concrete ones. Aesthetic as well as social criteria are applied to housing design and layout; this is particularly noticeable in Peter Willmott's comments on Dagenham. It is taken for granted that physical health and survival are important goals. The inherent desirability of education as such, and of equality of opportunity for access to it, are assumed, though little is said (except, in a different context, by Peter Marris on universities) about what the content of this education should be. Family relationships also seem at some points to be regarded as having an absolute and

13

inherent value: the desirability of a close relationship between husband and wife is stated, not argued;[3] Michael Young and Patrick McGeeney state as a matter of principle that '. . . parents have the right to be informed about what goes on in the school which their children attend and consulted about what should be done there . . .';[4] Michael Young, in a talk on planning, starts off 'I imagine we should all agree that one thing we do want is to create the conditions in which family life can flourish. . . .'[5]

It is hard to distinguish this kind of value premiss from arguments that family relationships should be promoted because people like them, but it is important that this distinction be made, since the two ideas imply quite different policy rationales: one rests on the assumption that people should get what they want, and the other on the assumption that they should get what the planner wants, or thinks will be good for them.

We may describe the value system as a whole by saying that it is one which takes for granted the desirability of health, education and family life; the vast majority in British society would no doubt agree, so that to take this for granted hardly appears controversial. At the more intangible level, the values expressed are less highly conventional, though by no means novel. They emphasise the importance, in every possible context, of respecting the individual's choices and allowing him scope to put them into practice, and use individual satisfactions and preferences as an ultimate standard; at the same time, however, not every choice that individuals actually make is approved. The fact that most inhabitants of Dagenham don't seem to object very strongly to its design is not held to excuse it from criticism;[6] the contentment of the people who live in Woodford with their way of life is treated as complacency, while no such criticism is implied of the contentment of people in Bethnal Green.

It is hard not to feel that these evaluations are a rather ordinary, if paradoxical, product of class attitudes: the university-educated upper-middle class condemn the lower-middle class for striving so hard after the advantages that they themselves can get without striving, while they can respect working-class people, who are sufficiently different to be interesting and whose values accidentally coincide on

14

some points with their own.

To describe the Institute's values in this way is only in a limited sense to criticise them. More serious criticism can be made on grounds of their internal consistency. We shall consider in turn a number of points at which there seems to be some kind of inconsistency.

Firstly, where individual preferences are being discussed in relation to social policy, rather than to purely private choices, the possibility must be raised of individual preferences conflicting. This creates an issue at two levels. At the level of general policy, a decision must be made between uniformity based on majority preferences and diversity which allows scope for minority preferences too. At the level of individual decisions, it is possible that one member of a family or other social group prefers one solution and another member another; there is no way in which general policy can resolve the difficulty if, for instance, a mother wants to live near her daughter but the daughter doesn't want to live near her mother.

It is evident that, if preferences are to be taken rationally into account by the planner, it is not sufficient simply to find majorities; their size, and the size of minorities, must be known, and so must the distribution of different preferences through groups in the community. This sort of problem has been recognised verbally by the Institute,[7] but their research has not usually been in such a form that it could help to solve it; localised samples give no clue to the total frequency or incidence of any phenomenon, and their findings tend to be presented as descriptions of majority situations which are attributed to the group studied as a whole.[8]

It is in connection with the value attached to education that many of these inconsistencies arise. As Peter Willmott hints in the passage about Dagenham quoted above, traditional working class communities and value systems are not usually very sympathetic to education, and even where it is seen as a desirable goal their pattern of life is such that it effectively handicaps their children for educational achievement. Thus there is something sociologically odd about combining the advocacy of education with a desire to maintain traditional working-class family patterns. Peter Marris recognises this when he describes the culture of

15

Bethnal Green as 'indifferent to education and hostile to ambition',[9] but this is in an article of general reflections; such recognition is not worked into the structure of the relevant books, and so no resolution of this tension is suggested.

One way of resolving it might be to change the character of the schools, and Peter Willmott indeed suggests that curricula might be made more directly vocational in order to hold the interest of teenage boys;[10] he does not consider whether such changes might not be so significant that the education given should no longer be classified by his own value system as desirable. Michael Young considers the idea that the values of the school need not be preferred to alternatives, and faces the problem of vocationalism,[11] but does not really suggest how the conflict should be resolved. In both his books on education he advocates involving parents much more in the schools, both as an end in itself and as a means to other ends. Implicitly, despite the democratic rationale, he must be assuming that where there is conflict the values of the school will dominate, since it is obvious that he is not in favour of many of the things that parents may want. Many groups of parents, for instance, have pressed for the retention of highly selective schools, and for conservative teaching methods. It is really not sufficient to say that both parental participation *and* certain kinds of educational reform are desirable; as when someone argues for capital punishment for murder on the grounds that human life is sacred, one must ask how it is proposed to reconcile the two ideas. A meta-principle which specifies the relative weight to be attached to the more limited principles is required.

More generally, one may question whether the Institute's support of working-class family patterns can be made consistent with other values that they hold. Initially, there is a logical oddity about advocating so strongly the continuance of a mode of life which they themselves interpret as a necessary response to past adversities rather than a freely made choice. Peter Marris recognises this in another article, saying:

Our view of working-class London was, perhaps, a little sentimental. We noticed the warmth, the disparagement of

16

individualistic self-seeking, the emotional ease, rather than the economic determinants which had matured their way of life.[12]

Equally, one may quote from 'Family and Kinship in East London' itself to show that the authors were aware of the potential dysfunctions of the patterns they describe:

This moral code which surrounds kinship is sometimes harsh, imprisoning the human spirit and stunting growth and self-expression. . . . (p. 162)

But, despite these examples, the general impression conveyed by the oeuvre as a whole runs overwhelmingly the other way: the weaknesses inextricably linked with the strengths of working-class life are played down if they are treated as such at all, and the effect is to create an inconsistency with other values the authors hold. A closely integrated local community is never likely to provide a milieu in which diversity and individual idiosyncrasy can flourish and be regarded with toleration; a community that draws its solidarity from shared adversity is not likely to be able to retain this solidarity when times are less hard, let alone simultaneously to encourage its members to take up opportunities to depart from the old patterns; keeping up an intricate pattern of extended-family relationships may be inherently incompatible with a close 'joint' relationship of husband and wife;[13] and so on.

The members of the Institute have thus been caught in two widely shared dilemmas. The first is the classic liberal dilemma of being in favour of democracy in principle, but also having strong views, which may not be supported by the majority, on what should be done. The second is the dilemma of favouring two policies each of which seems desirable in isolation, but which in practice are sociologically incompatible with each other. These are both painful dilemmas; if more is to be gained than some interesting insights into the torments of the liberal conscience, and in particular if consistent policy recommendations are to be made, some way out of them has to be found. No outsider can instruct the Institute on how to do this in ways that will best satisfy

17

their own principles.

It is only fair to add that there is some evidence in their published work of a trend over time towards more explicit consideration of these problems, so that this is perhaps one point in particular where it is not justifiable to treat the body of work as a whole. Michael Young's 'Innovation and Research in Education' and Peter Marris and Martin Rein's 'Dilemmas of Social Reform' raise some of these problems, as do also some of Peter Marris's articles. It may be significant that these are works which stand rather apart from the Institute's main tradition so far, and thus do not address themselves directly to the same issues. It means rather more when, in the most recent book based on Bethnal Green, Peter Willmott says, talking of some of the changes that had taken place in the ten years since they did their first research there,

> Bethnal Green is becoming part of the wider society.... The East End ... has always catered for the tastes of its immigrant minorities, but this is something different: it represents an extension of local horizons and of freedom of choice. ('Adolescent Boys of East London', p. 9)

This more critical detachment is to be welcomed.

Substantive Policy Recommendations

We come now to consider the policy recommendations made on the basis of these value judgements; our concern will be more with the logic of their derivation than with precise content. The recommendations made by the Institute are normally based in some way on their own immediate research carried out for that purpose, so substantive points can be made about particular policy recommendations, and methodological ones about the ways in which these are derived from the data.

Taking the value standpoint as given, there are two criteria for a good substantive policy recommendation: (i) it should be likely to achieve the desired effect — and equally or more likely to do so than any alternative which satisfies our second criterion as well; (ii) its costs (financial, psychological, social)

18

should be less than the benefits anticipated from it or, at worst, less than the costs anticipated from the best alternative. What constitutes a 'cost' is relative to the values of the person making the judgement; one man's costs may be another man's benefit. (The assessment of costs and benefits of course entails taking into consideration the ways in which other ends may be affected by the means chosen, and some decision has to be taken about the time span over which the assessment is to be made. Are short-run costs acceptable as the price of long-run benefits? This should depend in part on the degree of certainty with which the benefits are expected.)

It follows that the questions to ask when considering the merits of a recommendation are: does it seem likely, on the basis of available information, to achieve the desired effect? are there any alternatives which seem likely to achieve it better? what are the direct and indirect costs that it will entail? and how, in terms of whatever rate of exchange between different things may be devised, do these costs compare with the anticipated benefits? We shall attempt to comment on the answers to such questions about the recommendations made in some of the Institute's books, chosen from those with the most marked policy orientations.

The chief recommendations of 'Family and Kinship in East London' are that more housing should be provided in central city areas, and that where people have to be moved from old areas they should be given the chance to move as social groups rather than as isolated nuclear families. These recommendations follow from the stated general principle that people should have 'as much choice of residence as possible' (p. 155), and the finding that most people in Bethnal Green wanted to stay there, or at least in close proximity to members of their wider families or social circles.* Given the premises, these recommendations would obviously be likely to achieve the desired effect of proximity and it is hard to imagine any alternatives.

If, however, the findings were to be interpreted as showing that it was not necessarily proximity in itself that people wanted but merely many of its usual consequences, the

---

* The validity of the argument obviously rests on the correctness of this finding. This is a methodological question, and all such questions are reserved for the separate chapters on research methods.

desired effect might be achieved by other means. Swift, cheap and convenient public transport might be an excellent substitute, since it would decrease effective distance; a much more elaborate system of welfare services, and the provision of large numbers of nursery schools, might make the services exchanged within the family so much less important that proximity no longer mattered to people, at least in relation to other advantages; an increase in average levels of education and the provision of many adult classes and more diverse leisure activities might alter the interests and increase the independence of Bethnal Greeners to the point where other kinds of satisfactions replaced the traditional ones for which proximity is a prerequisite; and so on.

Whether any of these possible alternatives could achieve the same effect better can hardly be discussed without further and more detailed study. (We may note, however, that the fact that the book does not consider any possible alternatives is partly attributable to the use of survey data, which restricts the range of alternatives considered to those put forward by the respondents.) We pass on to the question of costs.

Some of the social costs of the proposed housing policy are considered in the book. Building more houses in central city areas would entail reserving fewer open spaces, and probably also moving railway yards out of the centre and constructing multi-storey factories. The only cost comparison made is implicit in the argument that people would prefer to have fewer open spaces if that was the only way to get more central houses (p. 165); this implies a comparison in terms of the extent to which people's preferences are satisfied. There is no discussion of relative financial costs, and so no consideration of what financial price would be worth paying for the anticipated social benefits; but this point only matters if the policy suggested would be significantly more expensive than current practice. However, it seems likely that the consequential abandonment of the points system for the allocation of new housing might bring other preferences, for perceived justice in the criteria used, into play. This problem could only be overcome if good cheap housing ceased to be a scarce resource, which was not probable in the foreseeable future at the time of writing.

20

Subtler costs are more interesting, and here there are so many possibilities that only a few chosen at random can be listed. If proximity successfully supports the maintenance of the Bethnal Green mother—daughter relationship, daughters will continue to take the advice of their mothers rather than of doctors about children's illnesses, and thus the children will receive inferior medical care. If proximity successfully maintains the old community spirit, it is in consequence likely also to maintain a lack of openness to ideas from outside the community, and harsh social sanctions against those who develop idiosyncratic interests or higher educational aspirations. If the pattern where real social relationships are confined to family and near neighbours is perpetuated, in extreme cases this may produce what Kerr calls 'role deprivation'[14] and in less extreme ones it is still liable to give rise to limitations on social competence that restrict the individual's range of choice in many ways. All these possible consequences would, I think, be regarded as undesirable by Young and Willmott. If it were established that they actually were inseparably linked sociologically with the desirable aspects of traditional working-class life, it would seem much less self-evident that policy should aim to support the continuance of the latter. Such potential indirect costs certainly need to be taken into account; a rational choice betweeen policy alternatives would require that sets of linked consequences be weighed against each other, although obviously every conceivable consequence cannot be taken into account. (Young and Willmott might still advocate the same policies after going through this process.)

In Peter Townsend's 'The Family Life of Old People' a far larger proportion of the whole book is taken up by policy discussion, and the suggestions made are correspondingly more detailed. Firstly, it was found that a sharp drop in income on retirement made it very hard to maintain previous interests and social relationships (p. 165); it was therefore suggested that a less literal definition of subsistence was needed and that pension levels should be raised. The bed-ridden and housebound had many special needs; these could be met in many cases by relatives, but old people don't like to accept help which they cannot repay, so special allowances should be available for those with these extra needs (p. 197).

21

Old people are much happier when cared for by their own families, and the families are willing when this does not place too great a strain on their resources. Policy should aim, therefore, as far as possible to keep old people in touch with their families, to support the families in looking after them, and to provide family substitutes where no relatives are available. The social services both could and should not try to replace the family, partly because the burden would be too great and partly because the great majority of people prefer family care (p. 202).

All this means that housing policy should provide small houses with gardens rather than flats for old people, and that these should be close to their relatives (p. 196); it also means that there should be more domiciliary welfare services to help the family. Where old people are in institutions, they should be allocated to ones in their home areas, and their community ties should be maintained by improved staff effort and in particular record-keeping (p. 201). For those without relatives available there should be a home visiting service, boarding-out arrangements or special accommodation with a resident housekeeper or warden, and greater attempts should be made to give institutions a family atmosphere (p. 198). Finally, old men have the special problem that retirement deprives them of a major role and interest; work has been the foundation of their self-respect and of the respect they receive from others even within the family. It is suggested, therefore, that subsidised workshops for the mobile and light work at home for the housebound should be provided, though this would not be economically viable (p. 151).

The whole trend of these recommendations is that whatever will make life happier and easier for old people should be done. Cost is not discussed, though it seems clear that the services proposed would not make spectacular differences to the standards of living of old people, even if they would greatly increase their elementary comforts. The proposals may be regarded as conservative in two ways. Firstly, they do not suggest radical changes in the whole position of old people in society. It is conceivable, for instance, that a really large increase in pensions — say to the level of average earnings of men in full-time employment — would make the provision of many public services superfluous, since pension-

22

ers would then be able to provide for themselves out of their own resources, buying what private enterprise had to offer. Conceivable though this may be, however, it is so far from the pattern of established policy that it would hardly be politically practical even if the true costs to the community were no greater.

Perhaps a more serious sense in which the proposals are conservative is that they take the pattern of life in Bethnal Green absolutely as given. Apart from the question of how representative Bethnal Green is, this prevents consideration of whether it might not be better to change Bethnal Green rather than public policy. This question is particularly hard to avoid when the problems of old men in retirement are being discussed. That old men should cease to be respected within their own families when they lose the status of wage-earners suggests to me that it would be desirable to change the values of the family rather than to invent artificial ways of keeping the old men earning wages — especially when even the most uneconomic schemes would still be beyond the physical capacity of many. That old men should have so few interests outside their work, and so little idea of how otherwise to occupy their time, again seems inherently undesirable and something that policy might usefully attempt to change rather than accept. To change these things would be more difficult than changing pension rates; the means could probably not be devised without further research into the causes behind them, and it would be too late for the existing generation of pensioners. But in social policy, as in medicine, in the long run prevention seems better than cure.

As far as the effectiveness of the measures proposed by Townsend is concerned, most of them respond in such a very direct and obvious way to a perceived problem that it cannot be questioned. The provision of sheltered work for old men, however, might raise difficulties; might not the very fact that it was known to be sheltered destroy much of its psychological value? This could only be answered conclusively by experience, but a more detailed study of the meanings of work and wages to old men and their social circles could lead to a reasonable prediction of the answer.

Financial costs could be estimated for Townsend's proposals if they were specified more precisely; but it seems clear that to him any likely cost would be offset by the social and psychological value of the benefits to old people. Whether the complete set of costs and benefits would be preferred to the alternative sets implied by different possible uses of the same resources of money and manpower is not considered; the argument is absolute rather than relative. In terms of widely shared values it would be hard to designate a more deserving group of recipients,* and it can never conclusively be argued that any particular other use of the resources is *the* alternative one, so it would be hard to say exactly what would be sacrificed by choosing this use.

Another kind of cost, however, can be located unequivocally, and that is the personal cost to the relatives of the old people of looking after them. This cost might be negligible; the norms in favour of family care might be so strong, and the social contacts with elderly relatives appreciated so much, that the time it took and the tasks and constraints it entailed were not really felt as disadvantages. We do not know whether this is so, and could not know without research on the old peoples' relatives as well as the old people themselves. It is certainly reasonable to raise the issue, and if there are such costs they should be set against the benefits.

It is possible that people don't like looking after the elderly, but would prefer family care for themselves in their own old age. This would not create a problem if there were a direct reciprocity of the same services at the same time between the same people, so that self-interest led to direct exchange; but what actually happens is that the old provide some reciprocal services of a different nature for the younger generation, who (in principle) follow the same pattern later on when they in turn have become old. Townsend's proposals implicitly, by planning to support this generational continuity where it might otherwise spontaneously lapse, introduce the idea of doing what is good for people rather than what they may currently prefer.

We move now to consider a much later book in the series, Ann Cartwright's 'Patients and their Doctors'. Her general goal is to improve standards of medical care and patients' satisfaction with them, and to achieve this goal administrative

* Though those who argue that the old should have saved through their working lives in order to support their retirement would disagree.

24

arrangements must be appropriate and both doctors and patients must be motivated to behave in appropriate ways. The broad recommendations that emerge are that a more critical milieu should be provided for general practice, that liaison between different branches of the health service should be improved, that G.P.s should be trained in ways that provide a more suitable introduction to the tasks they will face and be given better equipment to do them with, and that more preventive care should be undertaken (ch. xii).

At the more specific level, the following suggestions are made: (i) G.P.s who feel many of patients' complaints are trivial should be given the possibility of redress against the unreasonable by the setting up of some sort of grievance machinery (p. 62); (ii) the proportion of consultations taking place at patients' homes should be cut down by providing transport to the surgery, or by providing nurses to make home visits to simple cases (p. 76); (iii) G.P.s should be encouraged, and given financial incentives, to organise regular check-ups for people over 65 (pp. 96-8); (iv) the provision of courses to keep G.P.s up to date should be increased and made broader in scope and more interesting, and attendance should be encouraged (pp. 183-5); (v) a comprehensive campaign should be undertaken to educate patients to make the best use of their doctors (p. 224); (vi) appointments systems and partnerships should be more widely used (p. 167); (vii) research should be done on the development of new methods of evaluating standards of patient care, and on the consequences of introducing other suggested changes (p. 217). When some of these other changes had been made, it would become feasible to introduce quality controls, a system of incentives for good practice and thus a career structure in general practice; similarly, administrative reforms that led to a clearer definition of the job to be done by the G.P. would make desired changes in medical education and in patients' behaviour easier (p. 225).

These recommendations are at very different levels of precision; it is hard to discuss the more general ones, since without further specification their implications cannot be clear. (This in no way implies that they do not contain good ideas.) At least one implication of several of the recommendations *is* clear, and this is that the total costs of medical services would rise. To favour giving G.P.s better equipment is rather like being against sin; but whether, given a desired level of medical care, that particular allocation of resources would be preferable to the alternatives could only be judged when the experimentation and research that Ann Cartwright advocates had been done. In financial terms the institution of check-ups for old people could only be justified if the early detection of illness made its treatment cheaper than if it were left to be discovered by deliberate consultation about symptoms at a later stage. The obvious justification is not a financial one but one in terms of the value to the individual of good health and early treatment.

Health is a matter where there is such a consensus on the desirability of high standards that it seems quite disturbing to discuss the allocation of economic resources to it in ways which imply that one might settle for less expense and less-than-perfect care instead of greater expense and the best possible care. But it must be faced that decisions of this kind are in fact made, if only accidentally or by omission, and that while total resources are limited and maximum standards of health and care are not clearly defined and static they must be. Like 'The Family Life of Old People' (*mutatis mutandis*) this book takes its goal (health) as an absolute value, though the actual suggestions made are modest and 'realistic' in their degree of departure from the existing situation. The unresolved discrepancy between the two implied principles remains a source of slight tension.

Some more specific questions may be raised about effectiveness in relation to detailed recommendations. Might the proposal to make medical training more directly tailored to the G.P.'s task not have unwanted side consequences? Unless it were compulsory for all medical students, the status system of the profession might still operate in such a way that numbers who ended up as G.P.s did not take that course. It may be (as Ann Cartwright several times warns) that G.P.s who behave in certain less favoured ways do so because of factors such as their basic personalities or social backgrounds, which would be unaffected by the proposed reforms; the problem would then be one of recruitment. (There is a hint that this sort of factor might be relevant in the finding that doctors in partnerships, and so with more opportunity for

26

outside stimulation, did not show more commitment to preventive care or to other recommended attitudes (p. 167). If a career structure were developed within general practice, this might have the unintended consequence of weakening patients' confidence in the doctors who occupied lower ranks within it. This lesser confidence might indeed be justified, but while such doctors legitimately remained in practice it could well be dysfunctional. These are some possible speculations about the recommendations made; none of them, however, imply radical criticisms.

The analysis of effectiveness has to be considerably more complex here than in the discussion of earlier books, since not only are there *two* groups of people whose preferences have been studied but there is also the logically independent goal of good health. In fact the preferences of the groups are given less emphasis than in the other books because the promotion of health is taken as the criterion of overriding importance for policy; preferences are considered primarily as factors to be taken into account by the policy-maker, and only secondarily as ends in themselves. One very good reason for this is the evidence that patients' preferences are not deeply rooted, but depend on experience — as is shown, for example, by their views on appointment systems (p. 157). What should be done if patients turned out to have strong preferences which ran counter to medically desirable practices is not considered; the issue is not sharply raised by any of the data, and perhaps it was rationalistically assumed that health is so highly valued that preferences would change if patients were given correct information. That seems optimistic.

The chief remaining point of interest in connection with the policy recommendations made is to do with the power position of the medical profession in Britain. Any recommendation likely to impinge on doctors' interests must take this into account, since the profession is highly organised and has an excellent bargaining position. I do not know what Ann Cartwright knew as she wrote about the likely reaction of organised doctors to her ideas; perhaps it would be sympathetic. But one of the disadvantages of the sort of survey done is that studying a sample of isolated individuals and their opinions cannot give the data on structure and organisation, or on the views of individuals in key positions of influence, that are needed to predict likely reactions and thus realistically to anticipate them in the suggestions made.

Michael Young's 'Innovation and Research in Education' has for its central recommendation that there be more of both, and that the two should as far as possible be combined and related to each other. More specific recommendations follow from this, some of them on the ways in which this should be organised and others on particular topics where research and innovation are called for. The main ones on organisation are that some experimental schools should be set up (p. 91), that L.E.A.s should have research and development departments (p. 112), that a number of institutes specialising in research into particular aspects of education should be established (p. 119), and that a Social Science Research Council be set up by the government to channel funds into valuable projects and the training of future researchers (pp. 122-4). Within this framework a great variety of research could be encouraged, some of which could be done on a very small scale and initiated by working teachers, with technical assistance and co-ordination provided. Eventually teacher training could incorporate some knowledge of research results and techniques, and this would be helped if more research were actually done in the colleges of education (p. 117).

Some of the ideas put forward for particular topics for research are: the nature of the processes involved in the introduction and diffusion of innovations (pp. 28-9); the possible development of more diverse forms of examination, and the predictive value that examination success has for other areas of life (p. 47); the characteristics of teachers (pp. 48-53); the possibility of solving some of the educational difficulties of working-class children by associating their parents directly with the schools, by evolving syllabuses that relate more directly to jobs and so make more sense to their parents, or by treating the children in class less as competitive individuals and more as co-operating members of groups (ch. v). It is suggested that the influence of fashion is strong in educational innovation, and this makes it especially important not merely that each innovation be systematically evaluated but that, at the same time, the possible 'Hawthorne' effects

28

produced by enthusiasm for novelty should be investigated.

Because of the kind of book this is the alternative policies, the ways in which those finally recommended could be implemented, and the likely consequences of doing so are discussed much more fully than in any of the other books. With so many interrelated topics to be covered the total effect is necessarily complex, especially as many suggestions are made tentatively and different possible value standpoints are considered. From this complexity, however, it is evident that Michael Young is very conscious of the range of ideological and practical difficulties to be faced, and of the interconnections among different aspects of the changes he advocates. It is for this reason that, given the structure of the British system of education and research organisation, he ends up by recommending a multiple strategy in which some reforms are made at the centre while others are left very much open to local and individual initiative and independent diversity. The total strategy, therefore, cannot fairly be considered either as a coherent and unified whole or as a set of completely separate possibilities.

However, there are certain points which stand out. First, there are two about their effectiveness in achieving the desired aims. Attractive as the idea is of involving far more people in research, some of them given special *ad hoc* training courses to equip them for it, this does seem likely to generate a lot of rather poor research. The more there is, the harder it is for anyone to keep up with it all and sort out the good from the bad; and so the more likely it is that much will remain uncriticised, and that the natural affection for one's own results and interpretations will lead to a confusion of conflicting views rather than an emergent consensus. Michael Young is not unaware of this danger, and some of his suggestions would help to avert it, but I think in his enthusiasm he gives it insufficient emphasis.

The other point about effectiveness is one raised by Stephen Cotgrove in a review of the book.[15] He suggests that Young has not made sufficient distinction between basic research and development. Many of the most valuable educational innovations have arisen from ideas developed in pure theoretical research but, he argues, Young's solution of close co-operation between the theoretician and the practical

29

innovator in the classroom has been shown in the physical sciences to inhibit the intellectual creativity of the theoretician, and thus lower his usefulness. (Young might perhaps reply to this by suggesting that the comparability in this respect of physical and social sciences would be a proper subject for further research. . . .)

If we turn now to relative rather than absolute effectiveness, and thus to the question of alternatives, there seems to be one major possibility to which Young pays little attention. As he himself points out, teachers are usually ill-informed about the results of the research that has already been done (p. 112). Some of the work he advocates on the characteristics of teachers might help to explain why that is so, and L.E.A. research and development sections might help to remedy it. But it does seem plausible to suggest that limited research of high professional quality whose results were widely disseminated might do more to improve educational standards than would more research at a lower level of professionalism and not very widely disseminated. If so, the same total resources could be better employed in dissemination; there is already quite a body of sociological and psychological work on communication and attitude change to suggest how this might most effectively be undertaken.

Finally, the eternal problem of costs must be raised. Obviously Young's recommendations would entail increasing the total resources allocated to education, but equally obviously this additional financial outlay could well be more than balanced by the returns in increased efficiency if action on the recommendations produced the desired effects. As far as non-financial costs are concerned, there don't seem to be any significant ones which have not been anticipated — except perhaps that continual innovation and experimentation might give rise to stress as well as stimulus for teachers, and so might need at least to be carefully phased. One possible side consequence, but on the benefits rather than the costs side, would be a likely trend to the recruitment of more lively and original members to the teaching profession. Young has even anticipated the objection that education is not necessarily a good thing, and suggests that some research be done which starts from that assumption (p. 55).

The four books discussed are in many ways very different,

30

so no general conclusions can summarise all the points one would like to make about each. Certain common elements nonetheless appear, and it is these that we shall mention here.

Firstly, none of them considers the justification at the societal level for allocating greater resources to the particular problems they are writing about, and thus whether the needs they study are not merely pressing but more pressing than others. An ideally rational model of policy-making would need to take this into account, although it is exceedingly doubtful whether those in power actually do so in more than a very informal, rule-of-thumb way.

But if we consider the Institute as a special sort of pressure group rather than as social scientists — and I think it is fair to do so, at least in this connection — then this neglect is excusable, and may even be a valuable tactic. The task of a pressure group is to press, to bring the objects of its concern to public attention as urgently and dramatically as possible and to demand that action be taken to alleviate the problems. It is not the proper task of a pressure group judiciously to weigh up the alternatives and to take all interests into consideration — though it may be politically wise to appear to do so to some extent. But there seems to be a deeply felt value judgement that 'human' costs matter in ways that financial costs don't, rather than a political calculation, lying behind the Institute's tactics. This distinction between different kinds of costs can only really be made when the financial costs are relatively small, so that either the diversion of public resources from other uses that is implied, or the other public and private costs incurred in the process of raising money by taxation, are insignificant.

This may in part account for the failure, which we have several times noted, to discuss the politics of reform at the level of interest groups.* If absolute statements of value are being made, such factors are irrelevant. However, the relative modesty of the reforms suggested hints that such practical considerations have in fact been taken into account. It could be that they are left implicit because of calculations that to make them public would itself affect the interested groups unfavourably; if so, this is another instance in which social science suffers.

* This is done very fully in 'Dilemmas of Social Reform'.

It would certainly have been valuable to have a clearer distinction between what is regarded as ideal and what is regarded as inferior but a necessary adaptation to practical constraints. A collective Institute of Community Studies Utopia would be extremely interesting — so far we have only a negative one from Michael Young.[16] Its function would be to make explicit the ways in which practical and political considerations had led to the toning down of the recommendations implied by the authors' values, and thus allow scope for other interpretations of these constraints. (Some of the value tensions and inconsistencies noted earlier might, however, make this a hard book to write.)

Such a Utopia would also give a coherent picture of a whole society and the interrelations among its parts, and thus help to fill a gap in the policy thinking of the Institute. Particular problems have been treated on an *ad hoc* basis, while the connections among them and the broader consequences of the proposed solutions have been given rather little attention. Unless, however, different parts of society are so autonomous that what happens in one part has no consequences for others,[17] these consequences of possible policy decisions must be evaluated for a full assessment of their desirability. (This would only be superfluous if the value system of the person making the assessment were such that no consequences for other parts of society could matter to him.) It would be ridiculous, as well as impossible, to explore every possible ramification, but responsibility should be taken for at least the main ones to which either the writer's or the general public's value system attaches importance.

The same sort of argument can be applied to causes as to consequences. A good prescription must rest on an accurate diagnosis. But the 'causes' of any complex social situation — that is, those circumstances without which it would have been different — are infinite. If, therefore, one wishes to affect it, there are a large number of different points which might provide appropriate leverage. Some of them will be more effective than others, some will be normatively more acceptable than others, some will be practically more feasible than others; those which would be most effective may well be impracticable or ethically unacceptable. Thus, for example, such a potentially practical solution to the problem

32

of inequality of educational chances for working-class children as their compulsory removal to boarding schools at an early age is not normally even considered.

But if a good choice is to be made, something approaching a full set of the major alternatives needs to be considered, even if many of them are immediately ruled out. Failure to do this may lead to the most effective solutions escaping notice, and is liable to produce an intellectual conservatism that defines causes conventionally, and limits the scope of the search for reform. In the case of the Institute this takes the form of leading to recommendations only about the social services and the most direct kinds of public policy, and thus an orientation to cure rather than prevention.

So far this point has been meant as a criticism, but there is an effective rejoinder to it in many contexts. This rejoinder is that while the sociologist who is studying a situation with purely academic motives can properly be required to include every aspect in his study, there is no point in the policy-maker wasting his time on aspects he has no hope of changing. As Peter Marris and Martin Rein point out, in their very interesting discussion of this and related issues, the sociologist's theory may not identify variables which the policy-maker can see how to deal with.[18]

I would argue, however, that despite the strength of this rejoinder it has two weaknesses. The first is that it often ignores the possibility of *indirect* policy action, as when steps are taken to solve the problems of retirement by improving educational standards rather than by postponing effective retirement. The second is that some problems may be insoluble, or at any rate insoluble without social change so major that it currently appears impracticable, but nothing is solved by ignoring such facts, and airing them might start processes which eventually made major changes less impracticable

Derivation of Recommendations from the Data

So much for the substantive recommendations made; we turn now to a briefer discussion of the methods by which these recommendations are derived from the data. Some comments on this will be made later, especially in the first chapter on 'Research Methods', where the need for effective policy to have data not merely on possible contingencies but on their frequency and incidence is pointed out. The central theme of what we have to say here relates to the Institute's strategy of basing recommendations on the results of surveys which concentrate on the consumer's viewpoint. This has been a fundamental policy, and its disadvantages may not be immediately obvious, so they will be discussed rather thoroughly.

There are three basic possible relationships between survey data and policy recommendations:

(i) The survey solicits respondents' opinions on what should be done, and the researcher simply summarises these opinions and passes them on to his readers. This implies that the researcher recommends that the opinions found should be acted on.

(ii) The survey collects data on respondents' general behaviour and attitudes in policy-relevant areas, rather than on their views on what policy should be. The researcher then recommends policies which are designed to conform to the preferences expressed and to facilitate the continuation of the observed patterns of behaviour.

(iii) The survey again collects data on respondents' behaviour and attitudes, but the researcher makes policy recommendations which, taking the behaviour and attitudes found into account, appear likely to produce the effects which he for his *own* reasons regards as desirable. (His own reasons might include a desire to maximise respondents' satisfactions.)

We shall consider each of these possible relationships in turn, and discuss the headings under which the Institute's works can most appropriately be classified.

The first relationship between data and recommendations, where opinions are summarised and recommendations directly based on them, assumes that the opinions of groups of consumers* can be taken as an appropriate guide to

* This basic strategy could also be used where the sample interviewed were 'producers' rather than consumers. The argument in that case would be slightly different, but since the Institute has not done research of this type it will not be considered here.

policy. I suggest, however, that this is only so when a very restrictive set of conditions are met. These conditions are as follows:

(a) That there are no other significant groups of consumers whose viewpoints differ. Other things being equal, if there are such groups an equally good case can be made out for acting on *their* opinions. (Non-consumers may be equally relevant.) But it may easily be impossible to act on both sets of opinions simultaneously, or impossible to do so without incurring costs that nobody wants; then action cannot be taken without introducing further criteria to compromise or choose between the alternatives.

(b) That these consumers' opinions are relatively permanent, and not responsive to possible changes in their circumstances. If opinions change fairly rapidly, it may not be practically feasible to change policies often enough to keep in step with them. If the opinions change with circumstances — if, for instance, they usually express dissatisfaction with the weak points of the current state of affairs — they may change again, and even *because* policy has altered to conform to them. Thus it is only if one can be reasonably sure that the opinions stated express general and long-run commitments that policy can be expected to succeed in coming into line.

(c) That consumers' opinions rest on a well-informed consideration of the causes of current problems, the possible range of alternatives for dealing with them, and the likely further consequences of adopting each of the different alternatives. If a wrong diagnosis has been made of causes, the solutions advocated will not have the desired effect; if the range of possible alternatives has not been considered, the best one may not have been chosen; if further consequences have not been thought through, the solutions advocated may have ramifying effects which as a whole create worse problems than the initial one which has been solved.

(d) That it is administratively, politically, financially and sociologically feasible to act on these opinions. If, for instance, they would require a radical diversion of national resources to one particular sector of the

35

economy, or a sudden and fundamental change in child-rearing practices, the fact that these hypothetical changes would solve a problem does not make suggesting them very helpful to practical policy under ordinary circumstances, whoever makes the suggestion.

(e) The conditions previously stated assume that the researcher or policy-maker is committed to a belief in the desirability of acting on consumer opinion. We must add to this, however, one of two further conditions. The first is that his commitment to consumer opinion is so strong that it outweighs any substantive views he may have himself on the issue that differ from those of the consumer. The second is that (by happy coincidence) he regards the consequences of acting on the opinions actually expressed as inherently desirable, harmless, or undesirable but still a price worth paying for the indirect consequences associated with them. (To state these alternative conditions is simply to spell out that it is logically odd to advocate acting on opinions unless one either shares them oneself or holds some other opinion which leads to the same conclusion.)

Unless the group of consumers studied is a highly specialised one, it seems rather unlikely that all these conditions will be met. If they are not met, other factors besides their opinions need to be taken into account. It is useful to specify these implications of this most extreme position, since this clarifies the meaning of less extreme ones; few researchers would consistently make such a naïve use of their data, but traces at least of this approach can be found.

The second possible relationship between survey data and policy recommendations is that the survey collects data on respondents' attitudes and behaviour (rather than direct opinions on policy), and policies are then recommended which the researcher thinks likely to be acceptable to the attitudes and to facilitate the behaviour. This sort of approach assumes that consumers' wishes, whether verbally expressed or only behaviourally implied, should be deferred to, but avoids the 'democratic' assumption that consumers know how these wishes can best be achieved.

Conditions (c) and (d) above thus no longer apply,

36

although appropriately modified versions of them of course still apply to the researcher's own opinions. Conditions (a) and (b) remain relevant, if for consumer 'opinions' we substitute 'attitudes and behaviour'. The problem of devising one policy to fit more than one set of characteristics persists, though it is much less severe when some scope is allowed for the policy-maker's initiative. The problem of potential change in the characteristics the policy is to fit remains as severe as ever, except perhaps to the extent that reported behaviour may be less volatile than expressed opinions. In another sense this problem becomes worse, for to devise policies to perpetuate existing behaviour patterns is usually given a 'democratic' rationale which assumes that those behaviour patterns are preferred and freely chosen; but this may not be so. At least the asking of opinions does not build in conservatism so directly, although insofar as opinions follow from current circumstances it may do so indirectly. It is dangerous to infer that wishes, especially 'real' (i.e. unverbalised) ones, are expressed in behaviour;[19] positive social constraints, and negative lack of opportunity, may prevent their expression. Condition (e) above again applies, *mutatis mutandis*: a researcher still rationally requires his *own* reasons for advocating policies intended to put his respondents' preferences into practice, and thus still has to make value judgements of his own.

In our third type of relationship, these value judgements are made much more openly; the researcher does not even purport to use consumers' preferences as his dominant criterion, but collects data on them for his own purposes. Thus the discussion of the validity of this sort of approach revolves around the issue of the rationality of the arguments used by the researcher rather than those of his respondents.

If his recommendations are to be effective, he must be able to make reasonable predictions about the ways in which people will behave in the future if each of the alternative possible courses of action are followed; in order to do this he requires not only information about how they behave at present but a *theory* about their behaviour — that is the equivalent in this context of condition (b). Condition (a) becomes a point about sampling: if the sample studied is not representative, it will not allow adequate predictions to be

37

made. Conditions (c) and (d) apply again with the researcher's conclusions substituted for the consumers' opinions; condition (e) is no longer needed.

Thus we conclude that, whichever of these relationships holds, a researcher *cannot* exclude his own judgements of value and of facts from the relationship between answers given by his respondents and the recommendations he bases on them, whatever he may wish, nor should he rationally try. Thus the third type of relationship described is to be preferred as the one that makes this most explicit, and so lays open the full structure of the arguments employed for consideration; the first type of relationship is the least desirable, since it either suppresses certain stages in the argument or omits them and so reaches its conclusion by logically inadequate means.

Most of the Institute's books appear to claim legitimacy for their recommendations in terms of the logic of the first kind of procedure; the value of respondents' opinions is generally taken for granted, and the researchers' own values are often not overtly stated. However, as we discuss elsewhere,[20] respondents' opinions have frequently been inferred rather than directly asked, which paradoxically has the effect of pushing the research towards our second type of relationship between data and recommendations. Elements of the third type also sometimes appear. It is hard to allocate any book wholly to one category, which perhaps indicates a lack of clarity about the reasons for which surveys have been done; the trend over time seems to me to have been away from the first and towards the third type, but without a full consideration of the implications.

Finally, this discussion has assumed so far that the consumer opinions elicited are about the policies to be chosen. But those asked for have usually referred to past or current policies rather than to possible future ones. To the extent that this is so they constitute even less of a logically adequate grounding for the recommendations made, which must really rest on the researchers' judgements. Thus their work becomes a sociology of diagnosis rather than of prescription and treatment, however the data are used. A sociology of treatment would need to deal much more with future possibilities and the means of implementing recom

38

mendations.

Another aspect of strategy that requires discussion is the concentration on *consumer* groups. The rationale of this seems to be that their views are commonly neglected and they are therefore treated unfairly or in ways that don't have the intended consequences. From any standpoint their views are worth knowing; but it doesn't follow that the views of 'producers' or of members of the general public aren't also worth knowing. This, however, is the conclusion that seems generally to have been drawn; Ann Cartwright's books, and perhaps also 'Living with Mental Illness', are the only ones that study other groups too. Bruyn puts the objection very neatly when he says:

... Without the perspective which comes from the description of subjective opposites in an institutional setting, a study is bound to serve the interests of social criticism more than the interests of objective analysis.[21]

Social criticism is a useful activity, and not one to be despised. But only on the basis of objective analysis can the means of dealing with the problems that it locates be worked out. The behaviour of one group may look very different from the perspective of another with whom they interact.

The only justification for confining research to the consumer could be that we already know enough about other groups; at the level of social science rather than 'general knowledge' this only seems justifiable on the traditional working-class assumption of a homogeneous 'them'[22] whom we know about because, as social scientists and their readers and thus middle class, we by definition *belong* to them. (This might perhaps be modified to the assumption that the books are addressed to the 'producer' groups of social workers etc., but this wouldn't really affect the argument.) There is no reason, however, to assume that such commonsense 'knowledge' is social-scientifically valid or comprehensive enough.*

The results of omitting to study other groups are that the description of a problem situation as a whole cannot be

* For a very interesting, if rather heated, discussion of many related issues, see A. Gouldner, 'The Sociologist as Partisan: Sociology and the Welfare State', in 'The American Sociologist', iii 2 (May 1968) 103-16.

achieved, and that the opportunity of acquiring further information about the causes of the problem, and about possible consequences of different solutions to it, is lost. It is possible that from the viewpoint of other groups the situation might not be defined as a problem at all, or that quite different aspects of it might be singled out for that status; to omit the other groups from the study is to beg the question of who, if anyone, is right.*

Conclusions

All these results cumulatively tend to produce an approach which is sentimental rather than realistic, and thus one which is weak as social science. The sentimentality is enhanced when, in the studies done in Bethnal Green, the quaintness and exotic unfamiliarity of the subjects of the research throws a glamour over behaviour patterns which the investigators' values might otherwise lead them to regard as constituting a social problem. This fits in with the lack of realism implied by a reluctance to discuss whether people always want what is for their own good, in whatever senses may be given to that expression, or to consider potential conflicts of interest between individuals or groups.

Thus we must conclude that the strategies adopted by the Institute in arriving at their policy recommendations have been those of the pressure group and the social critic rather than of the sociologist. The appropriateness of their data for the purpose, and the ways in which they purport to use them, are often dubious. The apparent logic of grounding recommendations on consumer opinions is not borne out by a closer examination; there is no way in which the researcher can legitimately attempt, or practically succeed, to use them as a substitute for the responsibility of making his own value judgements and assessments of empirical situations. This means that where they appear to be used in this way the researcher is actually introducing his own judgements more or less covertly. (Where, of course, he introduces his own judgements overtly

* The neglect of the work situation of bureaucrats and members of the 'caretaking' professions, and thus of its consequences for their clients, may perhaps be seen as part of the Institute's more general neglect of work as a subject.

40

his research results cannot be expected to resolve value disagreements with other people.)

But this does not at all mean that the books cannot serve a useful function. I am convinced that they have done much to sensitise the public conscience to the human consequences of social planning, and to draw the attention of the caretaking professions to important subcultural differences between themselves and many of those with whom they deal. It must always be easier to develop an ethos which takes one's own interests into account and ignores those of others, and perhaps planners and others whose jobs entail the manipulation of large numbers of people are particularly liable to do so. A reaction against this can be healthy, even if it goes too far and on its own is excessively partial. To have done this is no small achievement, and the fact that many of their insights have now entered the conventional wisdom at least of the anti-establishment does not make it less — indeed is itself evidence of their success.

In some ways it would be more appropriate to consider the meanings the books have had to their intended audiences than the precise detail of what they actually say; to the extent that they have made the kind of impact they wanted, their work has been successful. There is a place for work that puts across a general value-orientation, just as there is for work that sticks close to data and works through its implications systematically; the best and most effective work combines the two. The Institute of Community Studies has tried to make this combination, with increasing emphasis on the latter, and the attempt has been worth making.

41

3 Research Methods: The Old Tradition

If we were to construct a stereotype of the methods used in the typical book-length report of the Institute of Community Studies, it would go something like this: The survey was, of course, done in Bethnal Green, and the book opens with a picturesque and graphic account of the area in general and of the more striking aspects of the lives of the people studied. The subject is a problem of social policy, and the survey is concerned with those at the receiving end of it, in particular as it affects and is affected by their family relationships. The research director himself, with the help of one or two colleagues, conducted 50-100 intensive interviews, using a rather unstructured schedule with many open-ended questions. A team of hired interviewers, using a highly structured schedule with mainly closed and factual questions, interviewed a sample of 800-1000 respondents in a more superficial way. Some data of a rather impressionistic nature were also collected by other means, such as informal observation and asking selected informants to keep diaries. The approach is mainly descriptive, with no formal hypotheses; the data are only very tentatively used to construct and test possible explanations of the observed facts, and there is little overt use of multivariate analysis or statistical tests. The main burden of the argument is carried by quotations from interviews, and the few tables are used chiefly as illustrations of the points made in this way. The conclusions are not merely summaries of the data, but contain policy recommendations. The strong orientation towards social policy is confirmed by the references given, only about half of which are strictly social-scientific; the main traditions represented are those of social anthropology and of social arithmetic, with government reports bulking large.

This is a stereotype, but not altogether an unfair one; about half the books, especially the earlier ones, correspond
42

to it quite closely. If one is to talk about the series as a whole, it is hardly possible to escape the stereotype; it is more useful to treat books singly and then to see if generalisations emerge. Our discussion of methods will be divided between two chapters. The first will consider those books that conform more closely to the stereotype, which are probably the best-known, and will reach some conclusions about this general pattern of research; the second will consider the more diverse remaining books, and end with broad conclusions about the Institute's methods as a whole.

The distinction between methods and theory is bound to be to some extent artificial, but has obvious conveniences. In discussing methods precise technical issues like sampling and question wording will be considered, but the basic criterion of judgement used will be the appropriateness and adequacy of the methods employed for the making of reasonable inferences and the drawing of substantive conclusions on the subjects studied. (Research not published in book form will not be treated here, since it does not seem to raise any fresh issues.) Issues of a more clearly theoretical nature are reserved for Chapter 5.

These chapters may sometimes risk giving the impression of taking a sledgehammer to crack a nut, in the sense that small points of method are discussed in more detail than their importance in the work as a whole can justify. I have felt it better to err in that direction, in the interests of thoroughness and precision, than in the other direction, and have tried to keep a proper sense of proportion in making broad judgements on the books as wholes.

'Family and Kinship in East London'

The Institute's first book 'Family and Kinship in East London', set out to discover '... what happens to family life when people move to an estate' (p. xv). In the early stages of the research, however, Michael Young and Peter Willmott were surprised to find that '... the wider family, far from having disappeared, was still very much alive in the middle of London.... We therefore decided, although we hit on it more or less accidentally, to make our main subject the wider family' (p. xvi). Thus the book came to have a dual focus: half is concerned to describe kinship patterns in Bethnal Green, and half to assess the consequences for family life of the move made by some Bethnal Greeners to the new estate of 'Greenleigh'. This gives it a certain ambivalence, and perhaps means that each subject is treated less fully than it otherwise might have been.

Several samples were used: a general sample of 933 adults in Bethnal Green, drawn from the Electoral Register, and interviewed with short factual schedules by hired interviewers; a 'marriage sample' of 45 couples with two or more children under 15, drawn from the general sample, and interviewed at greater length and with a much less structured schedule by the researchers themselves and a colleague; and a similar 'marriage sample' of 47 couples interviewed in the same way, drawn from former inhabitants of Bethnal Green who had moved to Greenleigh.* The Greenleigh sample was interviewed twice, once in 1953 before the main interviews started in Bethnal Green and the second time in 1955. (By the second time the sample was reduced for various reasons to 41 couples.)

The general sample is clearly very adequate in size to give a broad impression of life in Bethnal Green, but the marriage samples, despite their greater homogeneity, are too small to be used more than impressionistically where there are any meaningful internal differences. Smaller samples were taken so that they could be interviewed much more intensively, and the rationale of restricting them to married couples with two or more children under 15 was that the people who had moved to Greenleigh were mainly couples with young children. This doesn't seem very convincing, though, as the authors report that only 48 per cent of the ex-Bethnal Green households in Greenleigh in the summer of 1953 in fact consisted of parents with two or more children under 15 (app. 1, p. 170). They do not give any information about the composition of the other 52 per cent, but this does suggest that it would have been more appropriate to take a general

* There was also a 'grammar school sample', which consisted of girls from Bethnal Green who had gone to grammar school in 1935-9, but very little use could be made of it, as only 24 out of 40 could be traced, and this took so much time that the idea of getting a similar sample of boys was abandoned.

44

sample at Greenleigh and then draw one matched on the relevant characteristics from Bethnal Green. As it is, any conclusions that are drawn from the differences between Bethnal Green and Greenleigh must be confined to couples with children below the school-leaving age, and it is possible that the effects of the move would not be the same for those in other circumstances. One might suspect, for instance, that those with young children would be most reliant on their relatives, and find it hardest (as well as most expensive) to travel any distance to see them. This point is only partly met by the demonstration that among married women in Bethnal Green those with two or more children under 15 have *not* more often seen their mothers within the previous twenty-four hours (app. 1, p. 172); these figures say nothing of the quality or significance of the relationship, or of the roles of other relatives, which are relevant to any assessment of the impact of the move.

One may also ask if there was any particular rationale for choosing to look only at people who had come from Bethnal Green on the new estate: none is stated. To the extent that Bethnal Greeners are typical of those whom council policy moves to new housing estates, the effects of this policy can be studied through them; but to the extent that they are no different from others, there is no reason to confine the research to them. It was obviously convenient to have all the London interviews within one borough, but distances within the East End are so short that this doesn't seem a very strong justification. The strongest reason in favour of a broader sample is that, without it, one can only speculate about the possible differences. One finishes the book with a strong impression, created by the general tone rather than by the specific statements made, that Bethnal Green is a rather special place; to the extent that it is, the policy implications of findings about it are limited, and so therefore is the appropriateness of the sample used.

Various other aspects of the samples also merit comment. The strengths and weaknesses of the Electoral Register as a sampling frame are well known; one inherent weakness, and one that follows from the way in which it has been used, are relevant here. Firstly, it is always slightly out of date, and so under-represents those who have recently moved house; this probably isn't particularly important here, but in conjunction with the characteristics of those people who are not eligible for inclusion, or do not complete the form, might have contributed to the apparent high stability of the sample by leading to the omission of some of the less stable. Secondly, when the Register is used every adult of voting age has in principle an equal chance of inclusion in the sample; this means that extended families with larger numbers of adults living in the borough have a proportionately larger chance of representation in the sample. Thus it is possible that the use of such a sample, without any special precautions or checks, may have led to an over-emphasis on the numbers of related people living in close proximity.*

The Greenleigh sample is used as a panel, being interviewed twice with an interval of two years in between, but there is also an attempt to approximate a panel effect in the research design as a whole: the Greenleigh sample were not interviewed before they left Bethnal Green, but the 'before' state from which they are presumed to have changed is taken mainly from the Bethnal Green samples, and secondarily from a few retrospective questions. For the comparison between Bethnal Green and Greenleigh to constitute an adequate approximation to a 'before' and 'after' design, the Bethnal Greeners used in the comparison must have the closest possible resemblance to those now at Greenleigh as they were before they left. How close is the actual resemblance?

Data are given which show that in 1955 the Greenleigh couples were older, and had more and older children; the authors point out that this is partly because this sample was drawn two years earlier, and partly because of the L.C.C.'s housing policy: '. . . couples with more children, who were on the whole older, were in general more likely to be overcrowded and therefore eligible for rehousing'.† Thus in gross demographic terms there is a difference which might be connected with the differences found between the two samples.

* If they actually share the same household, the danger is eliminated, since all those living at the same address are listed consecutively and only every 36th name was taken.

† App. 1, p. 170. Townsend in his book raises another possibility: '. . . If there were brothers and sisters at home or in the district a married child seemed more likely to move to a housing estate outside London. Youngest and only children (whether sons or daughters) tended to stay in Bethnal Green, and other children, particularly the eldest, to move out . . .' (p. 35).

Whether or not it is likely to matter could easily be seen by holding age or number of children constant when making other comparisons; there is no indication that this has ever been done.

Going beyond demographic comparisons, we also need to know whether those who moved to Greenleigh differed in any less tangible respects from those left behind. Perhaps those who lived in the most crowded conditions, or in the worst houses, had the closest family relationships because they needed the most help? Perhaps those who were prepared to move to Greenleigh were those whose ties were less close? These two suggestions point in opposite directions; if the latter were true, it would strengthen the book's argument, and if the former were true it would weaken it. Again no evidence is given either way, so it is not clear what we may conclude.

Obviously the ideal research design would have included 'before' and 'after' for two comparable groups of couples, one of which stayed behind while the other went to Greenleigh. Young and Willmott do not say why they did not try to interview some couples before they left; maybe the estate was complete by the time they started the research, and this made it impossible. The book gives the impression that some couples had moved much more recently than others, but we are never definitely told when the estate was started, or what the distribution was, within the sample, of time spent there. If it was too late to catch couples going to that estate before they left, it might have been wiser to choose another estate altogether. As it is, the past in Bethnal Green, which for some was as long ago as 1948 (p. 107), is compared with a present in 1955; seven years, given the major housing upheavals which Young and Willmott document, may have made a considerable difference. In addition, the past of the estate couples is in part described by their answers to retrospective questions, on such matters as how often they used to see their relatives; it is very risky to attach much weight to memory in this sort of context, particularly when any unfavourable judgement of the move may have produced stereotyping and exaggeration of frequency of contacts in the past.

The schedule of questions used for the general sample in
47

Bethnal Green was almost entirely factual; it covered household composition, a number of facts about relatives outside the household, some questions on past and present housing, which relatives were seen on the last Christmas Day, and classification data such as age, sex, occupation and religion for the respondent. There were no questions on attitudes or opinions, and none that referred to other people ouside the family; the great majority were closed and had correct answers. Consequently, the interviews took only 10-30 minutes. This does not give much scope for comment; we may note, however, that it is not surprising that friends should seem to play little part in respondents' lives when there were no questions at all referring to them. There are questions about friends in the marriage sample schedule, but it is possible that friendship patterns change through the life cycle and so they cannot be taken as representative of the whole population of Bethnal Green; there is even a definite hint that this may be so: 'Several people said they had possessed many more friends when they were single. Marriage and children made the difference' (p. 84). (This must refer to the marriage sample only, though no indication of that is given in the text.) In the marriage sample schedule itself there is the possibility of bias introduced by the fact that all the earlier questions are about family, so that respondents are likely to have been set in a familial frame of reference by the time they got to the later ones where friends could come in.

The only other comment to be made is that some of the questions are put in a rather leading way: 'What changes have there been ...' rather than 'Have there been any changes ...', and 'Do you spend less on smoking and drinking than you did in Bethnal Green?' rather than 'Do you spend more, about the same amount, or less ...'. Survey convention, for good reasons, requires that questions should not be phrased leadingly unless this in done deliberately, and taken into account in the interpretation of the answers; in these two cases the wording seems likely to have led to an overemphasis on changes.

The instructions to interviewers permitted them to interview a spouse, or a parent in the case of unmarried subjects, if the subject drawn in the sample was not available at the first call; this respondent was to be used as a proxy rather than a

48

substitute, and the schedule completed as if for the original subject. A second call to contact the original subject was only to be made if '. . . it appears that the proxy does not know the answers to any of the questions . . .' (app. 2, pp. 181-2). We are not told the proportion of cases in which proxies actually were used, and it may have been trivial, but in principle this is a dangerous policy to follow, since it assumes that a close relative can give just as good information. In the case of household composition, this seems self-evident; it is less so when the question is about when the subject last saw his father. It seems likely that wives would more often be alone at home when the interviewer called than husbands, and so more of them would have stood proxy. By Young and Willmott's own account it was common for husbands to see the relatives on their side without their wives, and spouses could lead lives that were fairly separate, so it is quite possible that wives would not know of all the occasions on which husbands had seen their relatives. This means that the finding that men apparently see less of their relatives (pp. 29, 49) might be an artefact of the proxy system rather than a true representation of what actually took place.

Although the questions on the general sample schedule were so exclusively factual and closed, the text of the book contains many apparently verbatim quotations and expressions of attitudes. This is because most of the detailed material used is taken from the marriage samples, '. . . in order to simplify the exposition . . .' (app. 1, p. 172). In their introduction the authors admit that the marriage samples are small and need not be representative, but justify the use they make of them on two grounds: '. . . partly because we are interested in individual people even though they may not be representative, and partly because this research . . . is merely the first of a series of family studies' (p. xix). If this is so, it is hard to see why the general sample should have been used at all. To collect data on such a large sample suggests that some importance is attached to numbers as such; if it is not, the appropriate strategy would surely have been to save the money spent on it for increasing the number of intensive interviews. But how much use is actually made of the general sample?

In the first part of the book, devoted to Bethnal Green, 12 of the 13 tables are drawn from the general sample, so from

49

this it appears to be used quite a lot. But 13 tables in 105 pages is not much in social research; it is more informative to consider the role of the tables in the whole structure of the argument. A close examination reveals that the tables, and any data on the general sample presented in non-tabular form, have a very minor role. If we take two chapters, arbitrarily chosen, we find that one on 'Mothers and Daughters' contains 2 tables and about 22 lines about the general sample, and 13 pages about the marriage sample; one on 'The Kinship Network' has 2 tables and 25 lines on the general sample, and 8 pages on the marriage sample. The marriage sample data normally consist of anecdotes and quotations from the interviews.

The technique of presentation may be analysed in more detail: let us take the 'Mothers and Daughters' chapter. It starts with an extended example of the way in which Mrs Wilkins's life is interlinked with that of her mother; she is said to be not untypical in that she lives near her mother and sees a great deal of her. A table is then presented showing that, in the general sample, from 30 to 55 per cent of married men and women had seen their mother or father in the past twenty-four hours; women saw more of their parents, particularly mothers. 'But the number of contacts is less important than their content . . .', so this leads into examples of the content of such contacts, showing how child care and meals are spread across households. Such sharing is easier if mothers are closer: a table from the general sample shows that women who live nearer to their mothers see them more often. The key role of the mother is documented by noting that 68 per cent of married women last saw their mother at her home, and only 27 per cent at theirs; this is followed by many anecdotes about the social centrality and emotional importance of Mum. It is argued that this is in part due to the important services that she performs, and anecdotes are given about the ways in which Mum helped during confinements, and about three exceptional cases where women were not on good terms with their Mums. Three pages follow of instances of other kinds of help. The possibility of friction is mentioned, and it is stated that '. . . The mothers represent tradition. . . . The husbands, we found, were the main upholders of progress against the claims of tradition. . . .'

50

Instances are given of conflicting ideas over childrearing, and in particular the tendency of grandparents to spoil children in ways that parents did not altogether approve. It is concluded that the relationship most stressed by the kinship system of Bethnal Green is that between mother and daughter: '. . . They share so much and give such help to each other because, in their women's world, they have the same functions of caring for home and bringing up children.'

Thus all the qualitative data are drawn from the marriage sample interviews, and only the barest skeleton of facts comes from the general sample. The usual procedure of illustrating the hard data with examples is reversed: the anecdotes are illustrated by occasional figures. But the figures only 'illustrate' the anecdotes in a limited sense, since they are not on precisely the same subject; in this chapter, for instance, they tell nothing about the content of interaction, only its frequency. They cannot tell anything about content, since no questions have been put to the general sample on it. There is no obvious reason why this could not have been done; it would have made the interviewing and the analysis somewhat more complex, but the results would have been very much more valuable, since Young and Willmott are clearly interested in quality as much as quantity. As it is, this interest causes them to lay far too much weight on the marriage sample.

Although some use is made of the general sample, I would be surprised if it were not overwhelmingly the graphic quotations from the marriage samples that make an impression on the reader's mind, and it would take a very alert non-professional reader to notice that most of the figures given do not exactly refer to the same group or topics. Thus it is particularly important to consider what weight can be attached to their precise wording, since we do not know recorded; the only reference I can find says merely that 'They are as far as possible reproduced verbatim . . .' (p. xviii). We cannot tell, therefore, how much weight can be attached to their precise wording, since we do not know whether there was any element of selectivity or memorisation by the interviewer. The authors say in their introduction that '. . . some of the people . . . were more friendly, more frank and more full than others, and therefore bulk larger in our account . . .' (p. xix). There is always a danger that especially

51

quotable passages will be unrepresentative, and they could be so systematically if the more articulate and picturesque respondents also shared other characteristics. Whether they do or do not we can only tell from figures showing the proportions giving different kinds of answers; in this book they are not normally provided. We do not know if they existed for reference by the authors, but they do not mention any procedure of coding and counting the answers to the open-ended questions, so presumptively they did not.

Another factor that intensifies the possibility of bias on some topics is that, beyond the basic schedule used, the questions asked of the marriage sample varied with each informant in accordance with what the interviewer felt worth following up; this means that exactly comparable data do not exist for all the couples, and since those who were more talkative are likely to have given more points to follow up it is again conceivable that a false general impression may have been gained.

It is hard to avoid feeling that the researchers themselves have been carried away by the human qualities of their data on the marriage sample, so that they have not really noticed that they are using it for unsuitable purposes. For Greenleigh, only the marriage samples are relevant, but the Bethnal Green one is heavily used for the general description of the community in the earlier part of the book too. It seems likely that it is not merely the greater warmth and expressiveness of full answers as opposed to ticks and circles which has produced this effect; the marriage sample was interviewed mainly by the authors themselves, and it is only natural that the people one has met personally in their own setting should make a stronger impression than those who are only observed at second hand. It is unfortunate, therefore, that the authors did not take the routine precaution of also doing a cross-section of the general sample interviews themselves.

It is perhaps partly as a result of the excessive concentration on the marriage sample that at the end of the book what has emerged is an ideal-type Bethnal Green family rather than a typology; passing references are made to differences, but they are not systematically developed (as is done very usefully by Townsend),[1] so that we do not learn what proportions of people live in the various family situations. An
52

analysis of deviant cases would have been particularly interesting theoretically, since it would have helped to elucidate the relative importance of cultural norms and of structural constraints in producing the observed patterns.

Although the book is primarily descriptive, some explanatory ideas are introduced. No specific initial hypotheses are stated, although there is an intriguing reference in an appendix (app. 8, p. 216) to an early hypothesis that was later abandoned. This suggests that there might have been other hypotheses in the authors' minds, but if so we are not told what they were. When explanations for the findings are suggested, they are typically not in any sense tested, maybe because the appropriate data are not available. The hypothesis, for instance, that the closeness of the relationship between mother and daughter can be accounted for by their similarity of occupation could in principle have been tested easily, by comparing the relationships of fathers and mothers with sons and daughters when their occupations were the same and different. Not enough occupations were actually asked to make this comparison feasible, but not even the possible differences between daughters who are single, married but childless, and married with children, are examined.

This is part of a more general imprecision, which is also reflected in the inadequacy of operational definitions. In discussing Greenleigh, they comment that 'This change from a people-centred to a house-centred existence is one of the fundamental changes resulting from the migration . . .' (p. 127). It would have been possible to devise a measure of 'house-centredness', but this has not been attempted; nearest to it are the figures given on television sets per 100 households — and here the whole of Greenleigh is compared with the whole of Bethnal Green (p. 117) (G.P.O. figures) instead of with those of comparable income and stage in the life cycle. Moreover it is not clear whether 'house-centredness' is meant to be negative, reflecting the absence of outside amenities, or positive, indicating a definite attachment to the house. Both ideas are present, and it is important for the drawing of policy conclusions that one should know which it is, or whether both occur. It seems not unreasonable to make such demands even of an exploratory piece of research, especially when full pilot studies were (very properly) under-

53

taken, so that these difficulties might have been anticipated.

Thus our general conclusion on the methods used in 'Family and Kinship in East London' must be a rather unfavourable one. It has many avoidable faults, the majority of which impinge directly on the accuracy of its specific conclusions and the validity of the general impressions conveyed. Whatever its virtues, they are not of method. But the authors themselves admit that it is impressionistic, and describe it as 'a work of apprenticeship in sociology' (p. xix); we must see how they learnt from their apprenticeship in subsequent work.

'Family and Class in a London Suburb'

'Family and Class in a London Suburb' follows on directly from 'Family and Kinship in East London'; having found a certain pattern of life in a solidly working-class area, Willmott and Young wanted to explore the similarities and differences to be found in a middle-class area. For the area to be studied, they chose Woodford; no special reasons are mentioned for choosing this rather than another similar area, but perhaps the fact that their colleague Enid Mills was living there (p. x) may have had something to do with it.

Broadly, they expected to find that relationships in the community would be less warm and friendly than in Bethnal Green, and more specifically it was expected that the mother-daughter tie would be weaker, that kin would be more widely scattered and there would be less contact with them, and that a larger role would be played by friends other than kin and by clubs and voluntary associations. Their actual findings were that the mother—daughter tie was still strong, and stronger than they had expected, but not so central in the lives of their respondents as it had been in Bethnal Green. Kin were more widely scattered, but cars and telephones made this less important than it could have been, and children still looked after their elderly parents when they needed it. The working class in Woodford fell somewhere between the Bethnal Green and the middle-class Woodford patterns, although there was a real social cleavage between members of the two classes in the community. The middle-class families had more developed friendships, and were much more active in volun-

54

tary associations.

Explanations are suggested for the main findings. It is argued that the strength of the mother—daughter tie persists, despite obstacles, because they share an occupation. Kin are more distant because middle-class careers typically require physical mobility, but substitutes can be found relatively easily because of the social confidence induced in part by a sense of class superiority. The working class in Woodford are vulnerable to pressures to become more like the middle class because they lack the defences against them provided by an integrated one-class community like Bethnal Green, with its ideology based on the labour theory of value.

The methods by which these conclusions were reached are broadly similar to those used in Bethnal Green; they will only be discussed in detail where they differ significantly.

Three samples were used: a general sample of 939, a marriage subsample of 44, and an old age sample. This last was drawn randomly from the lists of G.P.s in the area, and was designed to be comparable with that used by Townsend in Bethnal Green; after a 19 per cent refusal rate, it consisted of 210 old people. For the purpose of comparison it was obviously appropriate to draw samples in the same way as they had been drawn before; the only new issue arising here is about the ways in which the samples are used. (We may note, however, that very little use is made of the old age sample; most of the quantitative data on old people is drawn from those who came up in the general sample.)*

One focus of interest is on the relationships between old people and their younger relatives; ideally for this purpose one would like to have the accounts of each relationship given by both older and younger generations. A random sample of individuals cannot give this since father and son will only both appear in it by accident. The obvious solution to the problem is to sample relationships — in this case, families — rather than individuals. This is commonly advocated but seldom done, because of the many practical

* The instructions to interviewers (p. 139) reveal that the study started as one of old people only, but later was changed to take in all age groups in the area; thus the old age sample was interviewed, and the results were in part analysed, before the rest of the research was started. The authors state that some of the quotations are drawn from these interviews, but it is not clear which, so the extent to which it was really used cannot be judged.

difficulties that it would involve. How much a failure to do it matters will depend on the extent to which the random sample used provides representative equivalents for the missing role-partners of the individuals in it; that is, in this particular case, it depends on the extent to which the old people in the sample are representative of the parents of the younger people in the sample, and vice versa.

We cannot tell how far they are representative without more information, but given the high level of physical mobility in the middle class, and given the social character of the housing in Woodford, it is quite possible that they are not entirely so; if, for instance, children had been socially mobile, either up or down, the social characters of the areas where they and their parents live are likely to differ, and Woodford may not have sufficient internal diversity to represent all the areas. This shows a major methodological disadvantage of restricting research to one small area. Although it would hardly be fair to criticise Willmott and Young severely for such a common inadequacy, this does suggest that the attempt to kill two birds with one stone, by studying both a community as such and the family relationships of the middle classes in one piece of research, means that each is dealt with less satisfactorily than it otherwise might be. As far as the family relationships alone are concerned, a national random sample with all its known weaknesses might have been preferable.

We are not told anything about the contents of the schedules used in interviewing the old age and marriage samples; we might infer that they were the same as those used by Townsend for the old people and by Young and Willmott themselves for their earlier marriage samples. It seems probable, however, that they differed in some way, since the main sample schedule (given in an appendix) is not identical with the one used in Bethnal Green. One might be able to infer the broad outlines of its content from a detailed study of the text, but this need not be a very good guide, and could hardly be expected even of the professional reader.

The main sample schedule is similar to the Bethnal Green one in general character: that is, almost all the questions are closed and factual, and many of them elicit demographic data about relatives. There are, however, fewer of the purely

56

demographic questions, and some alterations. Occupations are now asked for all the relatives, a great improvement, since it makes possible a documented discussion of the relevance of class position. A question asking when the last visit from a relative was received has been added, replacing the earlier one about who was seen over Christmas, and there is a similar one about friends and neighbours. Opinions of the neighbourhood are also asked for, with five alternative statements offered for choice; the three substantive ones are 'I don't notice them much', 'They are very easy to get on with', and 'They are inclined to be stand-offish' (p. 157).[2] Given the nature of the statements, it is perhaps not surprising that 64 per cent chose the one saying they were easy to get on with (p. 103), since 'stand-offish' is a mildly pejorative term; this is a rather blunt instrument for testing the quality of community relationships. (But a blunt instrument is perhaps sufficient for comparison with Greenleigh, and it is used in conjunction with quotations from the intensive interviews.)

There are also an open and a closed question on 'class' identification; to have either is an improvement on asking only occupation, and to have both shows a fair degree of sophistication. It is unfortunate, however, that in the text we are not told clearly which of the answers are being used, although a footnote indicates that a higher proportion of manual workers called themselves middle-class on the closed question (p. 115). This finding may be an artefact of the particular wording, which offers three gradations of 'middle class' to choose from but only 'working class' below them. It is well established that answers to such questions vary greatly in response to small changes in wording;[3] and it seems possible that the relatively prosperous manual workers of Woodford would quite reasonably not place themselves in the bottom category, although they might well have identified with the working class if offered gradations within it. In the circumstances, it would have been wiser to place more weight on the answers to the open-ended question; we are not given full details of these, so cannot guess what kind of differences this would have made. However, it may be that the conclusion that manual workers in Woodford are drawn in this way towards middle-class patterns, and the suggestion that, as a rule, 'the more the middle class predominates in the district, the more working-class people identify themselves with it' (p. 115), rest on inadequate evidence.

The chief remaining difference from the earlier schedule is in the inclusion of a sequence of questions about voluntry associational activities, church attendance and frequency of visits to a public house or hotel bar. These are useful questions to ask in themselves, but the answers to them cannot really throw any light on differences between Woodford and Bethnal Green, since they weren't asked in Bethnal Green. It is probably for this reason that all the explicit class comparisons made are within Woodford. Implicitly, however, comparisons of a vaguer nature are made; the relevant chapter starts with a general description of sociability in Bethnal Green, which concludes that 'Sociability, in such a setting, needs no organization ...' (p. 87), and ends by saying that '... Woodford is certainly rich in social organizations' (p. 98). It is not clear, however, what weight can be attached to such a comparison, given that the data were collected in different ways.

Some respondents kept detailed diaries of their activities; we are not told how many of these there were, nor now they were chosen. The results are used only impressionistically.

The interviewing in Woodford appears to have been done in the same way as before, with the marriage sample interviewed by the reseachers themselves, and the old age sample interviewed at least in part by Enid Mills, Peter Marris and Peter Townsend (p. xiii). Again a large part of the argument is built around quotations from the intensive interviews; this calls for no fresh comment. The general style of analysis, however, can usefully be discussed in more detail. It remains open to the criticism of looseness of argument, as we may show by a few examples. At the end of the third chapter it is stated that '... we have established ... that, for young couples generally, kinship plays a far smaller part than in Bethnal Green' (p. 35). The chapter is seven and a half pages long, and contains two tables, one comparing the proximity of parents' residence and the other comparing the recency of contacts with mothers. The first shows that the parents of the Woodford sample lived significantly further away than did those of the Bethnal Green sample, and the second shows that they had seen their mothers significantly less recently.

58

The differences in the second table are not large, though statistically 'significant', and the authors point out that they seem less than one would expect from the data on proximity. But they do not explore this finding any further or attempt to account for it by holding other variables constant, although this could easily have been done and suitable variables are suggested by their own argument. Tables presented elsewhere in the book (pp. 78, 169) hold class constant, and show that the working class in Woodford fall between the working class in Bethnal Green and the middle class in Woodford on both proximity and recency of contact; the two variables are never cross-tabulated to show whether recency of contact can be *accounted* for by degrees of proximity. It would be arithmetically feasible from the data given (though admittedly not very probable!) that *all* those who had seen their mothers within the past twenty-four hours did not live in the same borough as her. One cannot legitimately use proximity to explain recency until this theoretical possibility has been eliminated.

Less pedantically, it would surely have been interesting to examine the effects of car and telephone ownership; one might expect that car ownership would increase face-to-face contact, and telephone ownership decrease it by providing a substitute. To find out whether this was in fact so would not be simply to explore the obvious, since it would provide clues to the *desire* to see parents: if those with greater facilities for doing so do not see them more often, attitudes may be presumed to have intervened; if those with greater facilities do see them more often, the problem is to explain variations in the facilities rather than in attitudes.

This is connected with general points about the adequacy of the data for their purposes. The authors say: 'We are also sure enough in our own minds that this evidence on [recency of] contacts understates the differences between the two places ... ' (p. 34). It does not seem to have occurred to them, as a result of their earlier research or of pilot work on this study, to alter their schedule so that quantitatively and qualitatively more precise and relevant data could be got from it. Once again the need is felt for less impressionistic data on the *content* of interaction with kin, and its meaning to the people concerned; that interaction is less frequent

59

need not mean that it is less emotionally significant, or 'plays a far smaller part' in their lives in more than a trivial sense.

Similar failures to use the techniques of multivariate analysis where they would be appropriate appear elsewhere, as do instances where no measure has been devised of a variable of central interest. The closeness of the mother—daughter tie is again explained by their common occupational interests, '. . . stronger than the interest shared by fathers and sons engaged in quite different occupations . . . ' (p. 127), but even now that they have occupational data it is not used to test the hypothesis. They do not seriously consider the possibility (hinted at in a footnote (p. 38)) that broad differences in the salience of kinship between Bethnal Green and Woodford might be largely accounted for by the well-known class differences in typical numbers of children; it is conceivable that the lives of people in Woodford are less involved with those of relatives simply because they have fewer of them. In the chapter 'Are the Parents Deserted?' it is shown that in Woodford parents above pensionable age much more often live close to their children, and it is inferred that they have moved in order to be close together. But these data come from the general sample, and they were not asked any questions about where they or their children had lived in the past; the only evidence that a *move* had taken place comes from 6 cases quoted from the intensive interviews. (The figures given on proximity could have arisen in a number of ways without a move to be together having taken place: for example, older parents could live nearer their married children because the children were older and had become able to afford the quality of housing available in Woodford, or because at the time their children married there were still suitable houses in Woodford while for younger generations the only new houses were further afield.) Again, the quality of the relationship between husband and wife is regarded as generally important, and used to explain the difference from Bethnal Green in the significance of the mother—daughter tie — '. . . it is by and large less important in Woodford because the relationship of husband and wife matters more . . .' (p. 76), but there is no measure of it, either formal or informal.

A major part of the book is concerned with differences between classes, and between communities in which different

60

classes predominate. These themes raise a set of issues that can be discussed together. Firstly, how is 'class' defined? It is done by occupation (the husband's for married women and widows, their own for men and single women), using the Registrar-General's classification; for most purposes the occupations are simply divided into manual and non-manual, which entails subdividing the Registrar-General's class III and counting the clerical workers, shop assistants, salesmen, insurance agents etc. in it as non-manual (p. 159). This is fairly standard practice and, although many objections to it can be made in principle, it probably provides a perfectly reasonable working approximation. But one *ad hoc* decision was made to which there are serious objections: 34 'foremen, inspectors and supervisors', and 14 people in marginal occupations such as policeman, telephonist and laboratory assistant, were classified with the manual group because 'In preliminary analysis . . . they turned out to be, in all sorts of ways, more like manual than non-manual workers . . .' (p. 160). This means that 48 people have been classified primarily by their *non*-occupational characteristics, while for the rest only occupation has been used. But if non-occupational characteristics had also been taken into account for the other 891, many of them might have been classified differently.

More important than the simple inconsistency of this procedure is the nature of the criteria used, given the thesis of the book. The thesis is that class differences account for many of the other differences observed; if the other differences are used *in order to define* class, it is hardly surprising that the two correlate — this is a necessary result of the procedure used. How much this matters in the particular case (i.e. how much difference it makes) depends chiefly on the proportion of cases classified in this way. We are not directly told how many of the sample were classified as manual and non-manual, but from the figures given in the book it can be worked out that about 355 must have been manual and 584 non-manual. This means that about 14 per cent of those classified as manual, and about 5 per cent of the total general sample, were classified by a criterion that is open to serious question. This is a sufficiently high proportion to affect comparisons, given that many of the class differences reported are not very large; it is also certainly high enough to affect the characterisation of the working class of Woodford. If all the awkward cases had been classified as non-manual instead, the gap between working and middle class in Woodford would have appeared smaller; on the other hand, the gap between the working class in Woodford and in Bethnal Green might also have looked smaller. ✕

Given this division of the sample into classes, what use is made of class in the argument? It appears surprisingly seldom, in view of its weight in the conclusions, in tables in the text, though these are supplemented by further tables in two appendices. Where the orientation is comparative, the comparison tends to be between Bethnal Green and Woodford, regarded as working-class and middle-class communities. This, however, is not strictly a legitimate strategy, since neither community is completely homogeneous in terms of the authors' formal operational definition of class: 18 per cent of the Bethnal Green general sample are middle-class,[4] and about 38 per cent of the Woodford general sample are working-class. Comparisons of this nature between whole communities can only properly be made if it has first been shown that the community context has an overwhelming effect on the minority class group, so that it is not distinguishable from the majority group.

We have no idea whether or not this is the case in Bethnal Green, since no data are presented which separate the classes there, but in Woodford the authors show that the working class usually falls between Bethnal Green and the Woodford middle class; it seems likely *a priori* that there would be analogous findings for the middle class in Bethnal Green. This means that a comparison between the working class in Bethnal Green and the middle class in Woodford would have revealed rather more marked differences than does the comparison between whole areas. Much of the analysis is too impressionistic to be precisely interpreted, but it does seem that the authors have frequently confused community and class. A systematic distinction between the two would have entailed dividing the Bethnal Green sample, and could have been assisted by comparing Greenleigh, as a non-traditional working-class area, with Woodford; Greenleigh in fact makes only one very fleeting appearance in the later book, which seems a wasted opportunity.

62

The main conclusions of the book attribute an important causal role to class, but it is not clear what it is *about* belonging to a class that is meant to have such broad consequences. 'Class' is such a sweeping concept that demographic correlations between it and other variables can be little more than a starting point in the construction of sociological explanations. The status of the occupation of a family's main earner correlates with the frequency with which he and other members of the nuclear family see their relatives, or with the likelihood that they will take an active part in voluntary associations: *why*? This question can only be answered by bringing in other variables, which either play an intervening role in the causal chain, or show that the correlation with class is a spurious one (i.e. that the effect is produced by something else which is associated with class for other reasons).

To explore these issues it is necessary at the theoretical level to spell out the steps in plausible alternative causal sequences, and then at the empirical level to investigate which of these is more correct by seeing which steps are actually present in the data. Thus one might argue, working back through a hypothetical sequence, that working-class people see their relatives more because they typically live closer to them; that they live closer to them because they have not needed to move in pursuit of job opportunities; they have not 'needed' to move because their job ambitions are limited because, given the level of their qualifications and the structure of opportunities, higher ambitions would not be successful; and their qualifications are low because the quality of the education provided for working-class children is poor. (Note that even this laborious analysis has not brought us back to the class membership of the generation we are concerned with, but to that of their parents; further analysis would be needed to specify possible connections between the positions of parents and children.) The correctness of this sequence could be queried at any stage. It falls at the first stage if even those working-class people who live farther away from them see their relatives more, or if they do not typically live closer to them than do middle-class people; it falls at the second stage if they live closer to them even when unemployed for long periods of time when jobs are available elsewhere, or when they *have* moved in pursuit of job opportunities; and so on.

Obviously any one research project would be likely to take some of these steps as given, and the ones worth raising questions about in this context are those earlier in the sequence. The standard technique for answering such questions is to observe the effect of holding the appropriate variables constant: in this example, to start by holding constant within each class the distance at which people live from their relatives. Willmott and Young do not do this. Thus they commit, by implication, the ecological fallacy,[5] since the implicit argument is that if working-class people as a group typically live nearer their relatives and see more of them it follows that it is those working-class individuals who live nearest who see them most, while those who live at the distances more typical of middle-class people see them at typically middle-class intervals. This is plausible, but it certainly doesn't follow, and could have been checked. Alternatively, one could suggest that the initial correlation between class and seeing relatives was spurious; this would be so if, say, work in the same industry rather than at the same status level were the crucial factor, and it just so happened that more of the working-class people worked in the same industries as their relatives. Social mobility is the only variable that the authors consider in this way.

These examples again make the point that multivariate analysis has not been sufficiently employed (or at least the reader is not given sufficient evidence of its employment). I have been unable to find a single instance in the book where the meaning of 'class' is explored by using it in conjunction with another independent variable; the only cases where three variables appear in one table are those where one of the three is location in Woodford/Bethnal Green. Thus at the end we still have only the authors' untested speculations on this, although it is a subject central to their interests. This is very hard to excuse at a time when the main formulations of the techniques of multivariate analysis had been published for a number of years,[6] and when Elizabeth Bott had set such an excellent example on the theoretical level on a closely related topic.[7]

Thus our overall judgement on 'Family and Class in a

64

London Suburb' must be that, though it improves on the authors' previous book, the improvement is not as great as could reasonably be expected, and that it remains open to many of the same criticisms. Both are written highly impressionistically, and do not make it very clear how far these impressions can be supported by hard data; both present technically weak analyses of their quantitative data; both fail to construct adequate operational definitions for major variables used in the discussion, or even to collect systematic evidence about them at all; both tend to confuse the study of a community as such with the study of particular aspects of the life of groups of people living in it. Much of this might be summarised by saying that they use survey method both poorly and for purposes to which it is inappropriate.

It is interesting that Peter Townsend's 'The Family Life of Old People', which was under way at the same time as the earlier book, and is in many ways very similar in style, avoids falling into a number of these traps. The data are again mainly collected by survey techniques, and are presented with many anecdotes and quotations; the author says that 'In presenting the results I have tried throughout to keep individual people in the forefront . . .' (p. 9). However, in a sample of 203 old people all the interviews were done by the author supplemented by one colleague, and were relatively intensive, though certain points were always covered. This combines the advantage of reasonable numbers (in a rather homogeneous sample) with those of unstructured interviewing. A careful reading of the text shows that the structure of the argument is not so dependent on individual anecdotes, which are used to illustrate and give meaning to the figures rather than as a substitute for them. The picture that we are given of the old people of Bethnal Green is not stereotyped or ideal-typical, but is one that shows the existence of alternative patterns depending on particular circumstances: '. . . the extended family adjusts to the number, age and situation of its members . . .' (p. xi); and we are given an idea of how it may change over time. The representativeness of Bethnal Green in relevant respects is discussed in some detail (pp. 207-9). Data were collected on the role played by neighbours, friends and clubs, and it is concluded on the basis of this evidence that the family is indeed of overriding impor-

65

tance in people's lives. Finally, the connection of the findings with policy issues is discussed, in the light also of other research, over several chapters, with detailed consideration of the extent of need and of possible policy alternatives and their implications. This shows that it is possible, though admittedly on a more limited subject, to adopt a humanistic and individualising approach without losing the advantages of rigour and precision of method.

Bethnal Green is again treated as a working-class community, but in this case with rather more justification, since only 3 per cent of the old men in the sample fell into the Registrar-General's classes I and II (p. 141), while 52 per cent were classified as unskilled; presumably the distribution of the husbands of the women would be similar, so internal analysis of class differences would have been impossible. Data are presented (p. 92) using the class of their children as a variable. Class is used to a very limited extent as an explanatory variable, and then the emphasis is on the norms of the community subculture; this may have come about by force of necessity, but it is sociologically plausible and reduces the importance of distinguishing the class positions of individuals.

The books discussed so far are those that launched the Institute and first defined its character, or followed directly from the first ones, and so they have been analysed in great detail. For the rest of this chapter we shall consider the later books more briefly, concentrating on those aspects that introduce new themes.

Later Books

The next book in the series was Peter Marris's 'Widows and their Families'. It was designed to investigate further the part played in people's lives by family relationships, in this case in a situation of acute stress and transition. The subjects are 72 young recent widows in Poplar, Stepney and Bethnal Green. They were all interviewed by the author, using an informal schedule whose questions were put in a flexible order. Answers were recorded on the spot, in note form except for '. . . the most interesting [which were] as far as possible verbatim . . .' (p. 6); the rest was written up later, and he

66

called back if any oversights were discovered.

On all but a small number of factual issues the data are used as a set of case studies rather than quantitatively, so the fact that attitudinal questions were not coded and this rather loose technique of interviewing was used does not matter much. The analysis is descriptive, and multivariate only to that end; the description, however, does not purport to generalise. As the author says, '... a sample as small as this does not pretend to be widely representative. It can only suggest some of the consequences of widowhood in a particular place, without determining how common they are ...' (p. 8). In this case, however, the 'particular place' includes Poplar and Stepney, and it is observed that there were no noticeable differences between the boroughs (p. 131); one wonders whether differences would have been found in other surveys, and what the implications are for the books restricted to Bethnal Green. One may have slight doubts about the accuracy of answers to questions retrospective to before widowhood about familial contacts, but obviously there was little practical alternative. (Ideally they might have been checked with at least one other member of the family; more simply but ambiguously the answers of women widowed for different lengths of time could have been compared. Perhaps the best feasible solution, though one that could have thrown no light on individual cases, would have been to compare the answers given with those already given by a matched sample drawn from the Institute's previous research.) Class is not used as a variable, but so few white-collar occupations appear in the sample that it couldn't have been.

In broad strategy this book is similar to Enid Mills's 'Living with Mental Illness'; these similarities are clearly brought about to some extent by the concern of each with relatively rare contingencies, which means that rather small numbers of suitable cases can be found within a short radius of Bethnal Green. Once this restriction is accepted, it follows that an epidemiological approach, describing incidence and imputing causes to it, is not feasible.* If this is not feasible, however,

* It would have been feasible if the studies had dealt with longer time periods, either by going back further into the past or by prolonging the study into the future; but this was ruled out by the size of the funds available, and would give rise to difficulties about comparability over longer periods of time.

one may wonder about the social-scientific value of doing the studies. For both theory and policy it is worth knowing what contingencies *can* occur, but the value of such knowledge is limited if one doesn't have a reasonable estimate of their frequency, or of the circumstances under which their occurrence is more probable. One reviewer criticised Enid Mills severely on the grounds that her non-quantitative presentation of 'melodramatic' data gave a misleading general impression.[8] But, as he also observed, the case approach shows a proper recognition of the limitations of the data.

The sample consisted of 86 patients (all those who could be traced and were co-operative) from Bethnal Green who were admitted to the mental hospital for the area over a period of two years. There are some indications that Bethnal Green does have some special characteristics in relation to mental illness, and it is not clear what other areas might share them; in a hospital all of whose admissions were drawn from the East London areas '. . . people born in the borough had, on average, been mentally ill for six years before their first admission to hospital, compared with two years for those born outside it . . .' (p. 87). This information could presumably have been got from the hospital's records before the survey was planned, and would have suggested that it was inadequate to confine it to one borough; but against this may be set the advantage of studying the situation of the mentally ill against the background of what was already known about family life in Bethnal Green.

In each case either the patient or his next of kin was interviewed, and in most cases it was both. This seems an excellent idea, and a technique that can be advocated in other contexts.[9] Perhaps it was only done in the first place because mental patients were expected to be unreliable informants, but it gives the perceptions of other relevant people about the process of mental illness, and is in fact used primarily to supplement the patients' comments rather than as a check on them.

The interview schedule contained many open-ended questions, whose answers appear only as quotations; the only figures quoted refer to matters of fact, used descriptively. An informal typology of mental patients in terms of their attitudes to their illness is constructed (pp. 60-1), but this is

68

not used any further or related to other variables. It seems unfortunate that the diagnostic classification of the patients is not really used at all; the emphasis on the meaning of the illness for ordinary social life is valuable, but it seems likely that this would have some relationship to diagnosis, and that an exploration of this would be of considerable use to practical policy. The book leaves the reader with the impression that 'mental illness' is one homogeneous condition.

The next book, Peter Willmott's 'The Evolution of a Community', reverts back to the subject matter of the Institute's earlier work. It looks at the long-established council rehousing estate at Dagenham, and compares it with both Bethnal Green and Greenleigh; the aim was to see whether the patterns of social life that develop on a settled housing estate resemble those in traditional working-class areas, or whether the dissatisfactions found in studies of new estates are more than transitional. Dagenham was chosen as the settled estate to be studied because it too is a part of East London, recruiting many of its residents from the East End, and because it is a notorious example of bad planning and so should show particularly clearly the social consequences of planning mistakes (p. x). The latter reason is not altogether consistent with the general rationale of the project, since it implies an extreme case, while a study of the character of settled housing estates in general should be based on either a typical case or a cross-section of types. As the research turns out, the dubious appropriateness of this choice in principle does not matter much, since the emphasis of the findings is on the way in which social relationships and preferences can triumph over physical constraints.

'General' and 'marriage' samples are used exactly as in the earlier studies, and there is an additional 'tenants' sample consisting of 20 long-term residents who had moved to the Dagenham estate in its early days. The marriage sample were interviewed by the author and a colleague, the tenants sample by the author and his wife. The schedule used for the general sample was very similar to that used in Woodford; we are not told what the differences were. The marriage sample interviews were again very flexible, and this time we are told that notes taken at the time were written up into a full report, including verbatim remarks, later. A similar strategy was used

69

for the tenants sample. The argument is again built up largely from quotations from the smaller samples — of the 30 tables given, 21 are in an appendix — and we are directly told that the marriage sample were unrepresentative of the general sample in significant respects (pp. 105, 130). It sounds as though the quantitative data played a greater role in the interpretation than this suggests, since the author says that he looked at a wider body of data, and examined whether correlations might be spurious, before deciding to include a given result in the text (p. 133); the reader, however, is not given the information that would enable him to form an independent opinion on the validity of a given interpretation. The only really exploratory cross-tabulations presented are the 13 additional tables in appendix 2.

The modified version of the Registrar-General's occupational classification is used again; we are not told whether it was rigidly applied, or whether marginal cases were dealt with as in the Woodford study (p. 15). This has some importance, since tables are given comparing 'white-collar' and 'working-class' groups in Dagenham and in Woodford (pp. 139-40).

An informal typology is developed (pp. 65-7) to distinguish perceptions of differing degrees of friendliness and sociability in the area, and the causes of the differences are examined in the following chapter. It turns out that the physical layout of the houses at least in part accounts for these perceptions. This finding breaks new ground in relation to the earlier studies, and suggests the usefulness of relating facts that can be elicited without questioning to those drawn from the interviews. In general, this book is a more sophisticated version of the basic model developed in the early housing studies; it improves on it in some ways, but has not overcome all its faults.

Peter Willmott's 'Adolescent Boys of East London' is the most recent of the books to be confined to Bethnal Green, and therefore merits special attention. It gives a descriptive account of all the major aspects of the lives of boys in the 14-20 age group, with a strong emphasis on the developmental process over these years. Insofar as it is not purely descriptive it is concerned to see how far vague generalisations about modern youth, and sociological theories of delinquency, fit these boys. The usual survey method was employed, supplemented by several other sources of data. The main sample was a random one, chosen by indirect means from the Electoral Register, of 246 boys aged 14-20. A fairly representative subsample of these also kept a diary of their activities for a week. About 20 'selected' boys (p. 4) (we are not told *how* they were selected) were also interviewed in more depth at the Institute, and these were recorded on tape. Finally, some use was also made of informal observation both before and during the main research, and of pilot exploratory work. It is not absolutely clear how this last was used, but I presume only to contribute to the researcher's general impressions and broad interpretations.

The study was confined to boys because they are regarded as posing more of a social problem to adult society than girls (p. 3). This is a reasonable decision to make with limited resources available, though it does have the unfortunate consequence at the theoretical level that the distinctive behaviour of the boys cannot be explained so adequately (since the undefined respects in which the girls' situations differ must be crucial), while at the descriptive level only half of 'modern youth' can be covered. The study design used age comparisons between different boys instead of following the same boys through the different ages; this is in some ways inferior, but this technical inferiority is convincingly argued not to have affected the results here (p. 4). Once again the only purpose that seems to be served by confining the research to Bethnal Green is for this material to be seen against the background of the previous books; the uniqueness of Bethnal Green is again implicitly denied, in this case by using material collected by other researchers in Stepney and Poplar as a supplement (p. 138).

The questionnaire used in the main interviews was comprehensive in scope, and quite highly structured. There are a large number of open-ended questions, many of which are about attitudes or opinions. There are also numbers of closed attitude questions, offering a restricted range of alternative answers; these usually come in conjunction with an open one on the same general subject. This is an excellent technique, combining the advantages of the two methods used separately, and is a great improvement on earlier practice. Much of its strength is dissipated, however, by the apparent failure to make *systematic* use of the answers to the open-ended questions. There is no evidence that any of the attitudinal ones were coded. This means that the reader, and quite probably also the researcher, does not know whether, or in what sense, the quotations given from these answers are representative; this erodes their value as evidence. It also means that we cannot use these responses as a check on the meaningfulness of the alternatives posed by the closed questions, since we cannot compare the two sets of answers.

The data are presented both in numerical form (22 tables in the text) and as the usual lavish quotations. A new difficulty in the use made of the quotations is that hardly any of them are attributed to a source; thus we do not know whether they come from a taped interview or from a questionnaire response, and if the latter, in answer to which particular question. This is perhaps not very important, since it would not be proper for the reader to attach much importance to any one answer in any case, and the researcher presumably had at least a well-grounded impression of the representativeness of each one.

It is more worth noting that the role played by the questionnaire data varies through the book. Many of the chapters are based very closely on it, but there are parts — on attitudes to Bethnal Green, on sexual experience, and the whole chapter on delinquency (pp. 15, 21; chs iii, viii) — which are almost completely independent of it. It is to be regretted that these subjects weren't covered in the questionnaire. Despite the delicacy of sex and delinquency as topics, it has frequently been found by other researchers that it is by no means impossible to include them in interviews, and the interviewers were all young men in any case, which would have reduced the level of embarrassment. However, there is no misleading of the reader, since the text makes the status of the data used on these issues quite clear. A statement is made at the beginning of the book on the conventions which are followed: broadly, these are that only statistically significant figures are presented, and that a speculative rather than a positive form of words is used when an interpretation goes beyond the statistical evidence (p. 5). The only drawback of this is that a reader who is not very careful is unlikely to succeed in bearing it constantly in mind while forming his impressions from what he reads. The researcher himself did only a few of the interviews, using the same questionnaire as the other interviewers on members of the same sample, so the extent of the emphasis on graphic quotations must be a matter of policy, not a bias encouraged by the interviewing procedure.

The analysis of the data is more formal and complex than in most of the preceding books. It is mildly multivariate, with age one of the main variables used, and with one exception (to be discussed below) there are no conspicuous instances of failure to use relevant variables. No table presented uses 3 or more variables simultaneously, but there are hints that such analysis has in fact been done. Some correlation coefficients are quoted, though the full matrix is not given.

Occupations are normally classified (following the Registrar-General)* as 'non-manual', 'skilled manual' or 'semi-skilled and unskilled manual'; this means that, for the first time in the series, some differentiation is made within the working class in Bethnal Green. It is found that there are sociologically interesting differences between these categories, whether they are applied to the occupations of fathers or of sons. However, this variable of 'class' or occupational status is used much less than it might have been. The only time it appears outside the chapter on work is in a table showing the relationship between the type of school attended by a boy and his father's occupation. One would have thought that its possible relationship to club membership, to family relationships, to social activities and to attitudes in general would have been well worth exploring. This would have made the argument more explanatory, rather than simply descriptive, and would have raised once again the question of the *meaning* of class membership and its relationship to community structure.

Another kind of differentiation is considered in the final

* But note that here (p. 103) it is the 1960 version that is used, while in earlier books it was the 1950 one. The notes to the Census 1961 Occupation Tables say that the classification has been completely revised, and among examples given of occupations that have changed are draughtsmen, postmen, lorry drivers' mates, technicians and roundsmen (p. xiv). This creates difficulties of precise comparison which are shared by any research using the Census categories. (For a more general discussion of occupational classification, see Chapter 5 pp. 120-5).

73

chapter, where a formal typology is offered that classifies boys into three types, called 'working-class', 'middle-class', and 'rebel'. (The appearance of class in the names given to two of the types is a little deceptive since, as we shall see, they are defined by answers to questions many of which are not in an obvious sense related to 'class' as used elsewhere.) This typology seems very valuable, in that it makes a coherent, simple and systematic summary of much that has gone before.

It could be more than this, and one naturally starts thinking about how it might enter, as cause or effect, into explanations of the patterns observed. But its relationship to any of the other variables is not described, and on a closer look the reason for this becomes apparent: they are almost all incorporated into it. There are almost no data left in the study that could be used to explain *why* a boy should fall into one of its types rather than another, or whose variations it could account for. Thus it can hardly be used as anything but a descriptive summary.* It is particularly unfortunate that both the boy's own and his father's occupational 'class' are used in it, since this makes it impossible to see whether, and if so to what extent, meaningful clusters of other characteristics do correlate with occupational status. It would have helped if the reader had been given the complete matrix of correlations between items which we are told about on p. 94; as it is, one does not even know whether the boys from white-collar backgrounds more often gave 'middle-class' answers to the 'deferred gratification' questions put in as an index of class attitudes.

This leads on to some further points about the construction of the second version of the typology. It is not stated how the choice was made to base it on scales of 'social class' and 'rebelliousness', or to include the particular items that go to make them up. Perhaps the decisions were made in the light of the correlations found between the items. One needs to know, since scores on complex scales don't mean much unless one knows how they have been derived in the first place; the text makes it sound (pp. 165-6) as though items

---

* In fact two versions of the typology are given, constructed by different methods (app. 4). Most of the points made apply to both, but the more technical ones refer to the second and more sophisticated version.

were included intuitively, on inspection. The 'social class' scale contains three types of item: those on the boy's occupational and educational background, several on the extent to which his life takes him outside the East End, and three attitudinal ones designed to tap his propensity to defer gratification. It would be very interesting to know the weighting which the principal component analysis gave to each item. In the absence of this information, it looks as though the correlation between the two scales could be to a considerable extent accounted for by the fact that the 'occupational class' (and three other) items appear in both. It is also possible, for the same reason, that the typology adds little to the knowledge we can get from the occupational items alone; findings of that nature have occurred in many research contexts.

To sum up, therefore, 'Adolescent Boys of East London' shows far more methodological self-consciousness than do most of the earlier books, and as a result it is technically much superior. But the new techniques have not always been used in the most instructive way, and some of the earlier weaknesses still remain.

Conclusions

The strengths and weaknesses of individual books in the 'old tradition' of the Institute have been discussed in detail above; in conclusion, we shall attempt to draw out general points that apply to this group of books as a whole.

A key characteristic which they share is that all the studies described either took place in Bethnal Green, or were planned to be directly comparable with those that did. The advantages of this are that a cumulative picture of the area from a number of different viewpoints is built up, and the experience gained in one study can be applied in the next. The disadvantages, however, seem considerably greater.

In the first place, Bethnal Green is not necessarily the appropriate setting for research which is meant to be about the problems of widows and old people, or the structure of the working-class family, rather than simply about what happens in Bethnal Green. The extent to which Bethnal

75

Green as a community or its inhabitants as individuals are or are not representative of people in other areas is never treated in sufficient detail to suggest how far one could reasonably generalise from studies carried out there; if one cannot generalise from them, they have very limited relevance either as ethnography or as guides to social policy. It is curious, however, that the Institute has never actually done a full 'community study' of the area. This is a pity, for such a study could have met the obvious criticism of those they have done by treating work, and men's family and leisure activities, more fully; it could also have investigated how far Bethnal Green can meaningfully be regarded as a separate and internally integrated community, and thus thrown light on the legitimacy of making this assumption in other studies.[10]

Each area studied is usually treated as a 'community', as a whole, and variations within it become rather secondary. But it is not at all clear that the 'communities' actually operate as such in ways that are relevant to the more specific subjects studied; in particular, the *individual's* class may be more important than the class composition of the area in which he lives. It is very probable that both make a difference, but they need to be distinguished; the analysis in these books frequently confuses the two, as when, for instance, a comparison of figures for the Woodford sample as a whole with those for the Bethnal Green sample as a whole is treated as a comparison between middle and working class. A study of the ways in which the class composition of areas brings about 'structural effects' would be exceedingly valuable, and there are hints of this in the Woodford book, but it remains to be done systematically.[11] If, on the other hand, one is concerned to study effects which do not relate to communities as such, there can be no justification for limiting the samples studied to such restricted geographical areas; a description or estimate of the incidence of a problem logically requires a random sample from the whole population in which this problem is found. (Ann Cartwright's books in the series are models in this respect.) The funds available may make this impossible, but at least broader areas of London could surely have been covered.

The failure to do even one true community study, while so often seeming to come near to it, probably follows from the

76

frequent ambiguity of purpose in the research done: both to look at working-class kinship *and* to study the effects of moving to new housing estates; both to look at middle-class kinship in general *and* to study the particular problems of middle-class old people; and so on. Fuller studies of either could probably have been done, although each might have been in some ways less interesting, if only one had been attempted at a time.

We have dealt with the 'sampling' of areas; the type of sample chosen within areas also raises significant issues. The strategy used in three of the books is to have one large sample interviewed briefly and formally, and a smaller one within it interviewed much more intensively and informally. The smaller sample consists in each case of couples with 2 or more children under 15, and is thus not a cross-section of the larger one. This could only be justified if the data collected on the smaller sample were used exclusively to characterise members of that category, but this limitation is not observed. Here the desire to make the findings in later books comparable with those in earlier ones has led to the perpetuation of an unfortunate mistake.

The ways in which the intensive interviews are used provoke two more major criticisms. The first is that the blurring of possible distinctions between groups leads to the construction of stereotypes rather than the more complex and differentiated picture which is usually closer to reality.* Whatever the value in some contexts of an 'ideal-type' strategy, it is a misleading way in which to summarise empirical data unless at least a majority of cases can be shown in some sense to fit the pattern it describes. It has the very particular disadvantage that it directs attention away from 'deviant' cases. If the purpose of the research is purely descriptive, such cases need to be included in a complete description; if it is also explanatory, the analysis of deviant cases is always helpful, and often essential, to a detailed understanding of the processes at work.[12] (These issues are discussed in more detail in the next chapter, pp. 118-19.) As it is, the impressionistic and anecdotal way in which data are presented tends to make it unclear on which precise evidence

* This point applies to some of the books much more than others, as should be evident from the detailed analyses.

77

the conclusions are founded, and thus how many cases (if any) can be regarded as deviant.

The second criticism is that the answers from the intensive interviews are used *as a substitute* for the inclusion in the general sample questionnaires of questions on attitudes, meanings and the content of interaction. It is really inexcusable to have put in so few questions about the subjects which, from the texts of the books, appear to interest the researchers most; having omitted them, it is inexcusable to use the other data as though that were an appropriate alternative. The vast amount of work done in the U.S.A. on questionnaire construction might as well never have existed. (If it had been used, more explicit and more adequate operational definitions of major variables would probably have followed.) This is also poor research economy, since it seems very wasteful to have such large samples on which to collect simple factual information when so little use is to be made of it.*

Thus we must conclude that many of the distinctive features of some of the Institute's best-known books are, from a methodological point of view, either unhelpful or positively harmful; further, there were feasible alternatives which would probably have been preferable for their purposes. There have been noticable improvements over time, but these have usually entailed jettisoning part of the tradition. Conclusions about the aspects of these books which are less distinctive must wait until the next chapter.

* As an alternative to the use of more sophisticated questionnaires, participant observation is a useful technique for the collection of data on attitudes and meanings. It is curious that, just as they have done no true 'community' study, the Institute has never made formal use of systematic participant observation, although it would seem very relevant to their whole orientation.

4 Research Methods: Newer Models

In this chapter we consider the remaining books, which cannot be fitted as neatly into one pattern as the earlier ones; in subject as well as in method they seem to reflect a broadening out of the Institute's policy into greater diversity among individual research workers. Where similar points arise they will not be treated again in detail.

The first book we shall consider is Peter Marris's 'Family and Social Change in an African City'. In some ways this belongs in the previous chapter, but its exotic locale and some consequential variations justify taking it here. It deals with the consequences of a slum clearance and rehousing scheme in central Lagos, and is meant to provide a comparison with the Bethnal Green—Greenleigh rehousing scheme. It uses four samples: the two main ones consist of householders in the central slum area and in the new rehousing estate in the suburbs, and the others are of individuals in a larger area of central Lagos and of householders on the mainland of Lagos outside the slum clearance area. The first two samples are intended to provide a picture of 'before' and 'after', though they consist of different individuals;* the third is to provide statistical data for a larger part of the slum area, and the fourth to illustrate conditions outside the slums. To have so many samples is rather confusing, and some are not much used, so that their purpose seems to have been to enlighten the writer rather than the reader; but it is too easy for the reader to suggest, with hindsight, that

---

* For the possible drawbacks of such a design, see pp. 46-7. The rehousing estate sample is not directly comparable with the Lagos one: '. . . the estate tended to attract . . . those who were least characteristic of the streets from which they had been moved . . .' (p. 100). The analysis properly makes this clear, and indeed it is one of the main findings of the research. This makes it necessary, however, to distinguish between the effects of slum clearance and of the change to the rehousing estate. A systematic typology of households would probably have helped in this.

resources might better have been less dispersed. Obviously the conditions for undertaking a survey in an African city are more difficult, and hard to anticipate.

One condition, that of language, must however be discussed. The slum and the rehousing sample interviews were conducted by the researcher himself, the others by his Nigerian research assistant and by hired interviewers. Not all the respondents spoke English, and where they did not a Yoruba interpreter was used and the research assistant recorded the answers (p. xiv). (Presumably he also later translated them). This means that, even setting aside the universal problems of translation, the data may have been blurred or made not quite comparable; but this doesn't matter much, since fine shades of meaning are not analysed and non-factual answers have not been coded. Perhaps more important is that the interpreter was Chairman of the local Residents' Association; the team of three sounds like a fairly intimidating combination of status and strangeness. What effect this may have had on the answers given to them cannot be guessed by someone without independent knowledge of local conditions; the author does not raise this issue.

The language question links up with another question of tactics, and that is of the comparisons to be made with Bethnal Green. The whole ways of life in the two areas are so different that any comparison implying similarities needs to be made very carefully. Peter Marris says that he has '. . . used the terms most familiar to an English-speaking reader. A specialised terminology would have tended to obscure the similarities between family life in Lagos and an English city, and its greater precision is not essential to the argument . . .' (p. xi). This is fair enough, though the value of such imprecise comparison seems very limited; in fact comparisons are hardly made in the analysis — Bethnal Green does not appear once in the index. But the general orientation implied is likely to distract the English reader's attention from the rather different meanings that such ideas as 'family' have in Yoruba culture.

At the more detailed technical level, there are not many comments to be made. The great majority of the tables are relegated to an appendix, and most of the text consists of the researcher's summary and interpretations of his data; direct

80

quotations are used relatively sparsely. We are not given the precise questions asked of any of the samples, although at least the hired interviewers used a fixed schedule, but only a list of the topics covered; these are mainly factual demographic ones, so question wording would be unlikely to matter much in itself. The tables in the appendix are descriptive, comparing different samples and subgroups within them.

The next book to be considered, again by Peter Marris, is 'The Experience of Higher Education', which was planned to supplement the Robbins Committee's data on numerical demand for higher education with some information about its content as it is actually experienced by the students concerned. A survey was done of about 100 third-year degree students* in each of three universities and one college of advanced technology. The universities chosen were Cambridge, Leeds and Southampton; these three were presumably chosen for their diversity, on the assumption that they would therefore represent all universities. We are not told that any more precise principle of choice was used. Marris says that the similarities between the answers given at the three were sufficiently great to justify normally combining the answers from them (p. 4). This procedure raises some problems. Since no formal criteria for the sampling of institutions are stated, it is not clear how far they can be regarded as representative; similarities in the answers given could indicate the inadequacy of the sample just as much as its adequacy. The universities chosen differ in age, prestige, size, region, range of courses and proportions of students in each course; whether they fairly represent the range of possibilities in these respects or others that may be relevant we do not know. It seems fairly certain, however, that they cannot represent the range of variation in *combinations* of such characteristics. This suggests that it would have been better to treat the sample as one defined by whichever of the variables characterising the universities seemed relevant at each stage in the argument; this would mean sometimes dividing it into students at northern and at southern universities, sometimes into students at universities of different sizes, and so on. This is sometimes done, using the division into arts and science, or those living in hall and those in

* Diploma students at the CAT were also included.

81

lodgings, but these are treated as factors characterising the individual student rather than his organisational environment.

A separate issue is how far the sample used may be treated as one that is representative of all individual students.* There is nothing in the information we are given which suggests that this is appropriate in principle. (The usual Institute appendix discussion of the representativeness of the sample is not included.) It might have been difficult at that time to get appropriate national information, but at least figures showing the distribution at different universities by sex and faculty were available.[1] It is common knowledge, in any event, that Cambridge has a sex ratio very unfavourable to women, which almost certainly means that they are under-represented in the sample as a whole; on the other hand, it has a high proportion of public schoolboys, who are therefore probably over-represented. Such points as this limit the formal representativeness of the sample, but in view of the homogeneity of attitudes found should perhaps not be emphasised too much.

What may have led to more serious distortion is the fact that only third-year students were interviewed. No evidence can be claimed to demonstrate their representativeness, and there is considerable reason to believe that students at earlier stages of their undergraduate career would differ in various ways. Firstly, not all students reach the third year; some universities and departments within them have quite high drop-out rates, although there are marked variations. The drop-outs and failures are highly unlikely to be a random cross-section, and their experience of higher education seems quite important. Secondly, those students who do stay the course frequently change over time; many of these were interviewed when they would have been well into the period of revision for their final exams. On the basis of my own experience I would suggest that at this stage cynicism, vocational interest and range of friends are likely to be at their highest; memories of earlier attitudes and motives are of course likely to have deteriorated, and been reinterpreted, to an extent proportional to the time that has passed. It does not, therefore, seem plausible to argue that third-year

* The author shows that he is aware of the problems here, but regards them as insoluble with limited numbers (footnote, p. 6).

82

students will be the best informants; the viewpoints of students still at earlier stages should also be relevant, and so for that matter should those of recent graduates. It would have been desirable, at a minimum, within a framework of the study done, to observe whether there was any noticeable difference in attitudes between interviews done at different times in the academic year, and thus slightly different stages in the student's career.*

The survey was done in a fairly straightforward way. The interviewing was shared among the author, some colleagues, and an *ad hoc* team of research students and faculty wives. The schedule used contained many open-ended questions, at least some of the answers to which were coded, and a number of questions on opinions and attitudes. Answers were recorded as nearly as possible verbatim, and many quotations are used in the text. Some subjects are discussed to which the quantitative data are only peripherally relevant, but in general they support and provide a reasonable basis for the argument.

The approach is sensibly multivariate, with the more obvious breakdowns by subject studied etc. made. (We are not, however, given full details of the classification of subjects into 'science' and 'non-science', or the other slightly different divisions sometimes employed. Other studies have found meaningful differences between humanities and social sciences,[2] so it is a pity that this division was not tried.) The only classifications made of the students that are not implied by the organisation of the universities are those by class background,† by sex and by marital/sentimental status (married, engaged, informally attached, unattached); we are not left with any constructed typology of student careers. For this to have been developed, it would have been necessary to undertake a more complex analysis of the data, which the numbers

* From this point of view it is particularly unfortunate that interviews at each university were done in a block over two months (p. 192). Conceivably, for instance, the higher participation in organised events found in Cambridge (p. 82) could be because the interviews there took place in the autumn term.

† This differs interestingly from the slightly modified Registrar-General's occupational classification used in other Institute studies, which, it is argued, does not make very useful distinctions at the middle-class level. The classification used is designed to distinguish between occupations usually associated with upper-middle- and lower-middle-class ways of life (p. 185). No particular evidence is produced to support this, but it doesn't seem unreasonable.

83

in the sample might have inhibited.

After 'The Experience of Higher Education' came Ann Cartwright's 'Human Relations and Hospital Care'; this is so closely related to her later book 'Patients and their Doctors' that the two will be discussed together. Both are mainly concerned, as their titles suggest, with the patients' perceptions of the social relationships involved in the organisation of medical care, and their consequences for the efficiency with which medical needs are met. In each the sample of patients used is a large one of individuals chosen randomly from a stratified national area sample. In 'Human Relations and Hospital Care' all members of the initial sample were asked if they had been in hospital at all during a recent period of six months, and only those who had been were interviewed. In each book a sample of general practitioners was also approached; in the first they were chosen randomly from the lists of doctors practising in the districts sampled, and in the second the doctor mentioned by each member of the patients sample as his G.P. was approached. This latter approach seems preferable, since it means that the comments made by the patient about his doctor can be related to the characteristics of that particular doctor.

The ways in which the two samples are used, however, differ somewhat: in 'Patients and their Doctors' the characteristics of patient and doctor are related, while in 'Human Relations and Hospital Care' the G.P.s are used only to get the views of G.P.s in general on the relationships between hospitals and general practice. For technical comparability of the two books data would have been needed more on the hospitals attended by the patients than on their G.P.s. It is a pity that no independent data on the hospitals were collected (though this would have been laborious, and might have met with non-co-operation), since this means that the patients' descriptions and opinions cannot be related to variations in the facts of the situations in which they found themselves, or to the opinions of other people. (The author on p. 38 regrets that she did not have data on the adequacy of ward staffing, since this means that when patients attribute lack of attention from nurses to their overwork it is not clear whether this reflects real overwork or something about the patients' attitudes.) Thus it becomes rather difficult to draw precise

84

policy conclusions, since policy changes might not affect the sources of the opinions.

Another factor which contributes to a certain vagueness in the policy implications is the rather small use made of the diagnostic classifications of the patients. Very detailed medical classifications are given, but their only quantitative use is to give a general description of the samples. In the hospital study, for instance, a table gives the differing lengths of time for which patients had been consulting their G.P. before he referred them to hospital (p. 16), and this is in the context of a discussion about the adequacy of his procedure; these figures seem to mean very little without also knowing the ailments from which they suffered. Again, it seems likely that the nature of the patients' desire for information, and their preferences in ward size, might relate to their medical conditions. These might also, of course, properly have affected the decisions that doctors made about them; a patient's complaint of lack of information, for instance, could look rather different if it turned out that his condition was one which anxiety might cause to deteriorate, and those responsible had judged that full information might provoke more anxiety than it allayed.* The only diagnostic category treated separately are maternity patients; perhaps this can be done because the diagnosis is so unequivocal!

Difficulties of accurate diagnosis apart, there are some strictly social-scientific problems here. A purely medical classification of conditions might in many ways be the most relevant at the point of policy-making, and would certainly be necessary whatever else was done; but to explain patients' attitudes and reactions a rather different kind of classification might be more appropriate, which would ignore medically important distinctions. Patients might, for instance, be classified by their degree of physical disability for ordinary activities, by the popularly perceived dangerousness of their ailment, or by the extent to which it was felt by other people to be an embarrassing one; any one criterion of this nature would only be relevant for a limited range of purposes. To work out and apply such classifications would make the research process much more complex, even if the results

* I do not wish to imply any substantive expectations about what would have been found if further analysis had been made; the point is purely methodological.

would undeniably be more valuable. A feasible way of getting such advantages without vastly larger resources would have been to stratify the sample by diagnosis, and limit it to a small number of complaints that seemed likely to differ in theoretically important ways; this would not seriously have limited the generalisability of the findings, since other complaints could subsequently be classified along the dimensions found to be relevant.

Despite this criticism, data have in general been collected by very comprehensive questionnaires, and are carefully analysed. In 'Human Relations and Hospital Care' no tables use as many as three variables simultaneously, and the answers to open-ended questions tend to be used as quotations rather than coded and counted; most of the multivariate analysis is rather oddly tucked away in separate chapters at the end. All these points apply less to the later 'Patients and their Doctors', which is particularly strong in its exploration of the *meaning* of the attitudes expressed — revealing, for instance, that patients' views on the desirability of an appointments system seem to depend largely on whether or not their present doctor has one. (This concrete example makes clear the danger of drawing policy conclusions from statements of preferences which are not further analysed.) No hypotheses are stated, but some very careful causal statements are made with full awareness of the causal ambiguity of correlations.

Both these books are distinguished from the Institute's other work by their heavier use of quantitative data, and more sophisticated manipulation of it; this probably stems both from Ann Cartwright's statistical training, and from the traditions of the field of medical research. The result is that the figures are sometimes so dense that it is hard for the reader to find his way through them all and come out the other end with a coherent impression. (Whether this is preferable to the opposite fault, and whether it is possible to avoid both, are discussed in our conclusion.)

In between these two books in the sequence came Michael Young's 'Innovation and Research in Education'; this, along with Peter Marris and Martin Rein's 'Dilemmas of Social Reform', is too different in genre to be discussed in terms comparable to the other books in the series. Neither of them

86

set out to be examples of sociology in quite the same sense. 'Innovation and Research in Education' contains the results of a survey, but they are only presented very briefly in an appendix and not worked into the text; the main body of the book is a review of research done by other people, with some policy conclusions drawn from it. 'Dilemmas of Social Reform' examines the reasons for the success and failure of various programmes for the attack on poverty, and does so in a fairly sociological way, but the method of collecting data and drawing inferences from it is not sufficiently systematic, nor described in enough detail, to be considered separately. We shall proceed, therefore, directly to a more detailed consideration of research method in the latest book, 'Learning Begins at Home.'

This describes the results of putting into practice one of the recommendations of 'Innovation and Research in Education', by undertaking an experimental alteration in a school. The attempt was to make it an experiment in the strict sense, with experimental and control schools and 'before' and 'after' measures of the dependent variable of children's attainment. What the experiment aimed to discover was whether children's standards of attainment could be improved by increasing their parents' interest and participation in the life of the school.

One London primary school, 'John Lilburne', was chosen as the experimental school; it was in a poor district with a fairly high proportion of recent immigrants, and near to though not actually in Bethnal Green. Before the trial period began, four sets of tests (on arithmetic, reading, verbal and non-verbal I.Q.)[3] were administered to the children there; these were repeated six months and a year later. During the trial period, a large number of innovations were introduced:[4] a letter translated into the appropriate languages was sent to parents from the headmaster; open meetings were held; parents were invited to private talks with their child's teacher; special meetings were held to discuss teaching methods; some home visits were made to parents who hadn't attended any of the meetings; special meetings were held for groups of immigrant parents. In addition to the test data on children, there were interviews with a random sample of parents before the trial period began about their contacts with and attitudes to the

school (chs 2 and 3), and 27 'case study' interviews after-
wards with parents who had come to meetings to find out if
these had provoked any changes in their behaviour (pp. 100
ff.). Obviously the variety of approaches used in the trial
period was so great that it was not feasible to investigate the
effect of each individually; the general strategy was to treat
them as a group.

Comparisons were made in terms of test results between
'before' and 'after' at John Lilburne as a whole, and between
particular subgroups of children — over- and under-achievers,
those whose parents came to meetings and those whose
parents didn't, immigrants and non-immigrants (ch. 6).
Comparisons were also made between John Lilburne and the
children at the two control schools where no experimental
innovations were made. Controls were unfortunately only
introduced into the design after inspection of the figures for
the first six months at John Lilburne, since these suggested
the possibility that improved scores might be due to test
practice, given that the same tests were used each time. In the
control schools, therefore, the same tests were given twice, at
intervals of six months, without any other form of intervention by the researchers (pp. 91-2). The two schools chosen
were other nearby junior schools, with similar class composition and proportions of immigrants; the late decision to
include them made any more exact similarity impossible to
achieve.

But far more serious obstacles to strict comparability than
this arose. The researchers' ethical code led them to let the
control schools know the test results immediately, and not to
make any attempt to prevent the Heads introducing changes
during the six months. Consequently, both Heads did introduce major changes as soon as they saw the test results; one
even successfully used the discrepancy between the children's
results on tests of 'intelligence' and of 'attainment' as an
argument to get two more part-time teachers! (p. 33) This, of
course, makes the comparison with the control schools
almost meaningless, and thus radically undermines the value
of the whole research. It is hard not to feel that it would have
been quite sufficiently good ethical practice to hold back the
first test results until the end of the six months; the whole
project would then have been improved, at the cost only of a

short delay before the Heads could act on the results.

The tests used were standard ones, and the full details are given in appendix 1 of the book. The authors treat them with a certain amount of scepticism, and their content will not be discussed here. The questionnaire used in the 'before' interviews with parents is given in appendix 2, and this will be considered briefly. It is mainly factual, with reasons for behaviour frequently asked; the open-ended questions usually ask 'Why?' or 'What happened then?'. Precodes for the closed questions are very simple, mostly of the yes/no, often/ occasionally variety; there is no evidence of formal coding of the answers to the open-ended questions. An odd feature is that every time the parents are asked whether they have followed the 'right' course of action those who turn out not to have done so are asked why *not*, but those who have done so are not asked *why*. This suggests that the researchers regarded the 'right' behaviour as self-explanatory, which is a rash assumption to make, especially in a population where considerable cultural differences are likely; it is consistent, however, with the general absence of questions on aspirations, and on their detailed perceptions of the school and its meaning to them. It is conceivable that if they had investigated further they might have found out that the 'right' behaviour sometimes took place for the 'wrong' reasons, and such information could be highly relevant to any attempt to change the behaviour. Another drawback of this pattern of questioning is that it is likely to have suggested to the parents being interviewed that the 'right' style of behaviour was the normal or expected one, and thus influenced their later answers.

The chief use made of the answers to this questionnaire, apart from the purely descriptive one, is to correlate indices of parental interest with their children's scores on the first batch of tests. There are a lot of graphic quotations used in the text for descriptive purposes. The schedule, if any, used for the follow-up case study interviews with parents who had attended meetings is not given, and the results are only presented in the form of quotations and brief summaries of the details of individual cases.

The quantitative analysis of the main body of data has been done with a fair degree of statistical sophistication: a principal component analysis is used on the interview data (no useful components were found (p. 146)), and a stepwise regression analysis was used to relate parental characteristics to children's test scores. This latter seems to be addressed to a very different audience from the rest of the book, for it is confined to an appendix and its meaning is given an exposition which would be very inadequate for anyone who did not already know something about it. (What the appendix shows is that 'family background' seems to account for much more of the variation in scores than do the 'parental interest' variables taken separately; this could have depressing implications which run counter to the optimistic tone of the book as a whole. It is a pity that we are not told which of the 23 items that went into the 'family background' variable had the greatest weight.) When comparative test scores are presented, results of statistical significance of the differences are always given.

The findings of the initial survey of parents confirmed those of the Plowden Report, showing that in general the children whose parents showed more interest and gave them more encouragement had higher test scores, although there were exceptions that complicated the issue (p. 40). But the central findings, those on the effects of the experiment, are hard to interpret. Average test scores at John Lilburne over the trial six months did improve significantly, and this improvement was still maintained at the end of the second six months. However, average scores *also* improved, and to a comparable extent, in the control schools, where the Heads had introduced changes in the teaching rather than in the participation of parents. This means that the improvements at John Lilburne cannot be attributed to the experimental programme; they might equally have been brought about by the unintended effects of the experiment on its teachers (pp. 94-5).*

This throws the crucial burden of proof onto the comparisons *within* John Lilburne. These show that attendance by parents at private interviews with teachers only correlates with significantly greater improvements in test scores on the

* Some sort of check on this could have been made if a measure (however informal) of teachers' enthusiasm had been devised, and comparisons made between the children in classes taught by different teachers.

reading test, and when the parent concerned was the mother. Attendance at the special meetings on teaching methods made little difference for arithmetic,* but children of parents either of whom came to the reading meeting did improve significantly more on the reading test; however, this was predominantly true for the second-year children, whose parents had also had written advice from the Head about how to help their children at home. We are not told that any variables other than attendance were held constant, so this evidence by no means demonstrates that the attendance was the crucial factor, as the authors themselves point out (pp. 99-100); the important variables might be those which led the parents to come or not to the meetings, rather than what happened once they were there.

It was to check on this point that 27 visits were made to parents who had attended either the reading or the arithmetic meeting (pp. 100-5). In 8 cases no changes at all during the trial period were reported. In the remaining cases 12 parents said that they had taken to giving their children active forms of help, and 7 mentioned less specific changes such as feeling 'more relaxed'; none of these changes could be clearly attributed to the meetings as such. It is not stated how these parents were chosen for home visits, but a check back to the details given about the relevant two meetings suggests that they may constitute 100 per cent of the families represented at them. But, however adequate a sample of attenders they may therefore be, conclusions based on such small numbers can hardly be convincing. It is greatly to be regretted that a proper follow-up study of a sample of the whole group of parents was not incorporated into the design. (The authors say that they would want this if they were doing another such study.)

Although the conclusions on the central theme of the book thus need to be, and when formally stated are, extremely tentative, it is quite clear that the investigators started out committed to the idea of the desirability of parental involvement, and remain so at the end. Indeed they make a formal declaration of partisanship, which is quoted in part in our chapter on values.[5] It is obviously to their credit

* The authors suggest (p. 99) that this may have been because the meeting on arithmetic was not so well run as the one on reading.

in the circumstances that they undertook to do research into the matter. This bias does, however, have the unfortunate consequence that some other aspects of their research which might have been followed up in detail are left unexplored, and many of the most interesting parts of the book are thus only at the level of speculation. If, for instance, they had not been so preoccupied with parents, it might have occurred to them that the research process would be likely to have some effect on the teachers, and some sort of measurement might have been devised which would allow this to be taken into account; then the inevitable doubt about the relative importance of changes in teachers' and in parents' behaviour might have been resoluble. As it stands, the data seem if anything to imply that the teachers were more important; the authors interpret it otherwise. A suggestive final chapter comparing national educational systems is in no way based on the data they collected, and the interesting points made about the resistance of teachers to various kinds of innovation are an accidental by-product of the research process.

We come now to our broad conclusions about the research strategy and techniques of the Institute of Community Studies. For the sake of clarity these will be put in general terms, although there may be some exceptions to the generalisations; these exceptions should be evident from the comments on particular books.

The Institute's methodological intentions were, and are, good ones: to combine the strengths of rigorous quantitative method with those of personal involvement and observation in depth. Unfortunately the result has often been to get the worst of both worlds, with data from each being used for purposes to which they are unsuitable: large samples have been asked inappropriate questions, so that the answers are of little use, while small and unrepresentative samples have been used for generalisations; survey data have been under-analysed, while personal anecdotes have been over-interpreted.

It is in part because of this that one receives an overall impression of a lack of demonstrable respect for *evidence* and its role in reaching conclusions; this need not imply that those conclusions are wrong ones, but merely that they are

92

not sufficiently convincingly supported by what appears in the text. We have already discussed the loose style of analysis that is commonly employed, and now summarise the major points not previously stressed that have contributed to this impression:

 (i) Where diaries kept by informants, or observation, are used, this is not done systematically, either in the selection of observations or in the analysis of the data; their status thus remains anecdotal.

 (ii) The answers to open-ended questions are seldom coded and counted, so that their function again appears to be that of providing anecdotal quotations rather than systematic evidence.

(iii) When quotations from respondents are given in the text their sources are often not clear, and the question to which they replied not quoted; thus information about the context in which the answer was made, which is relevant to any assessment of its meaning, is not available.

(iv) The analysis of the data presented is seldom really multivariate; most of the cross-tabulations are descriptive rather than analytic. If as many as three variables are included, one of them normally defines the sample. This means that the interpretations offered are often not tested against alternative possibilities, nor the samples broken down into smaller and more precisely defined groupings.

 (v) Key concepts in the analysis and interpretation often have no formal, or even informal, operational definition; sometimes no data that could be used for this purpose have been collected, even where it was (or could have been) known at quite an early stage that these concepts would be used.

(vi) Large amounts of information about the methods used are given in appendices, but it is not always on the subjects most relevant to an understanding of the data and an assessment by the reader of the interpretations made of it. For instance, at least one appendix mentions how the data were counted on punched cards; it is hard to see how this information could be of any value to the reader. On the other hand, the schedules used in intensive interviews, and for some other samples, are not given; nor are we usually told how the answers were recorded in intensive interviews. Both of these could have considerably more bearing on the meaning of the data presented.

On several of these issues, it is quite possible that the appropriate procedures have been followed, but the facts are simply not told to the reader. However, the books must be judged as they have been written: like justice, social-scientific evidence must not only be had but be *seen* to be had. The reader cannot properly have confidence in results arrived at by methods that are not clearly specified.

Problems of evidence, inference and proof are quite frequently referred to in the Institute's prefaces and conclusions, so it is clear that they are conscious of them:

> . . . we can only report what people say they do, which is not necessarily the same as what they actually do. ('Family and Kinship in East London', p. xix)
> . . . Our bias — in this context any belief is a bias — must have influenced the outcome of our research and may have led us to interpret our findings in such a way as to favour our thesis. ('Learning Begins at Home', p. 107)
> . . . Contact between patients and their general practitioner is usually sporadic. Some people hardly know their doctor, others have such a close tie that they may be reluctant to discuss it with a stranger. The questions asked may sometimes be ambiguous or inappropriate. Patients' statements may be inaccurate because of misunderstanding or poor memory. They may be misleading, either deliberately or through vagueness. Their opinions may be based on wrong suppositions or inspired by prejudice. Doctors too may not always answer questions fully, frankly and accurately. These are the common hazards of questionnaire studies, to be constantly borne in mind. ('Patients and their Doctors', p. 2)

To at least one reader, the cumulative effect of such remarks (and there are more in the same vein) is irritating

94

rather than placatory. It is excellent to recognise the problems, but that is only a first step; the next step is to employ the existing techniques, or devise new ones, to solve them. We have tried to indicate some of the places where this could have been done.

The particular issue which two of these quotations raise is that of the validity of questionnaire data. If there is one central methodological policy to which the Institute appears committed, it is the use of questionnaire surveys. Yet it is by no means obvious that this is an appropriate technique for every subject they have studied. If one is concerned to find out about behaviour, why not study it directly? How great the need is to study it directly, when there is a choice, will depend on the extent to which there is reason to believe that the true behaviour differs from what is likely to be reported; the likely accuracy of report depends on such characteristics of the behaviour as its recency, public or private nature, and degree of conformity to norms held by the respondent or attributed by him to the interviewer. (It seems possible, for instance, that the people of Bethnal Green held norms about family behaviour which, in the conditions of the 1950s, led them to unconscious exaggeration of the amount of contact they had with relatives, although this might have been an accurate description of some cases or of some periods in the past.) Thus we return again to the point that systematic observation, 'participant' or of some other kind, could have been valuable in a number of the Institute's studies; several also offered scope for the exploitation of administrative records.

Lastly, we come to a pair of issues that are closely related to those taken up again in the chapter on theory. In discussing most of the individual books we have referred to the nature of the classifications employed, and to the construction (or absence) of typologies, which are a form of classification. The form in which this problem has most commonly arisen is that of the classification of occupations into 'classes'; class frequently plays an important role in the descriptions and explanations given, but neither the theorising nor the criteria of empirical classification are sufficiently clearly worked out for precise implications to be traced.

The importance of classification is more than merely

technical: it is crucial to sociological understanding and explanation. It is probably safe to say that there are no sociologically interesting generalisations about all social groups, or all men in whatever social context they find themselves; for valid generalisations of more limited scope, groups and individuals must be divided into sociologically relevant categories. This holds whether the purpose is some immediate practical application, or the refinement of abstract theory. Within almost any group that may be studied there are likely to be meaningful distinctions to be made: the individuals in it have had different pasts, and so experience the present differently; they have different social characteristics and varying patterns of social relationships in the present; and they are at different stages in careers and lifecycles that give them diverse prospects for the future. To make summary statements about a whole sample tends to imply not merely that a majority, if not all of them, share certain characteristics now, but that they are likely to continue to do so in the future; to make more differentiated statements indicates the dependence of current characteristics on contingencies, and so is likely to imply superior predictions and explanations as well as more accurate description. This is the basic objection to a mode of analysis that glosses over potential classificatory differences, and finishes up with an 'ideal' (or more strictly a 'constructed') type as its end product. Even in the Institute's most sophisticated books those typologies and classifications that have been devised seem to have been put to rather little use.

The other matter of theoretical relevance concerns the kinds of sample that are employed. It has been argued that these have quite often been not altogether appropriate to the purposes for which they were intended; two further points in this connection may be added to those made earlier. Firstly, there is often implicit or potential in the arguments of the books the idea of structural effects related to the individual's membership of a community, a class, a family or an organisation; but the sampling is not initially done, or subsequently used, in such a way that these can be analysed. The distinction between the collectivity as an aggregate and as a meaningful social group is not made theoretically, and so the samples are not employed to explore the ways in which

96

individual behaviour varies in different social contexts. This is connected with the second point, which is that the custom of studying samples consisting only of 'consumers' inevitably gives a partial, if not actually biased, picture of the social relationships in which they are involved. The common element in these two points is that both rest on the assumption that the individual is only in a limited sense a sociologically significant unit, and that it is therefore necessary for a full understanding of his actions to collect data also about the larger social units to which he belongs.

These criticisms are severe, though I hope sufficiently documented; they have applied absolute standards, and so should not be read as implying that books from the Institute are worse than most others. It is because there is a substantial body of work there, with a certain standing, that it seems proper to apply the highest standards. Nor, however, do I think that the standards suggested are ideals which are impossible to achieve in practice, and belong only in textbooks; they all specify procedures which working sociologists have used with a reasonable degree of success. Most of these sociologists have been American; once again, it is a great pity that the Institute's researchers have taken so long to show signs of familiarity with the best American work in their field.

One suspects that some of the weaknesses have resulted not from ignorance, but from commitments to certain values and to a policy of putting them across to the widest possible audience. But this desire to popularise the results of social research does not have to lead to methodological over-simplification, although it may mean that the results have to be written up differently for different audiences. The convention that detailed technical matters are reported in articles in professional journals,* to which footnote references for those interested can be given in books intended for wider audiences, is an established and viable one. If this convention were followed, the sometimes rather uneasy mixture of professionalism, condescension to the layman and excessive simplification could probably be avoided. The Institute's

* Numbers of articles on research done at the Institute have been published in professional journals, but they have not been of this nature.

97

methods have shown some marked improvements more recently; let us hope that these will be sustained and further developed.

5 Theory

It is common in sociology to distinguish between theoretical and descriptive research.[1] One may doubt whether pure description without any tinct of theory is possible, at least within the scope of a piece of work of finite length, but certainly the distinction refers usefully to differences in the purpose and design of research. Different criteria are therefore relevant in the discussion of research which is mainly descriptive and research which is mainly theoretical or explanatory in intent. It is usually taken for granted, however, that both are necessary to the complete discipline of sociology, though within it the description is done in order that in the long run theory may be advanced; even for those temperamentally more interested in description theory is economical, since it throws light on cases not yet studied.[2] Thus it seems appropriate to discuss the theoretical aspects of the work of the Institute of Community Studies despite the fact that the main aims of most of the books are not theoretical.*

Their interest in policy makes this all the more relevant, since if policy is to have the desired results it must rest not only on a correct description of present states of affairs but also on a correct understanding of how they came about and of the likely consequences of making possible changes. If further justification were needed, it would lie in the fact that the books have now entered into the public domain of 'the literature', where other sociologists with different interests make use of them. We shall attempt, therefore, to outline their ideas in the major substantive areas of middle-range theory[3] that they have been concerned with, and to consider

* The only two books whose central intention is in some way theoretical are 'Family and Class in a London Suburb' and 'Learning Begins at Home'; 'Family and Social Change in an African City', 'The Evolution of a Community' and 'Adolescent Boys of East London' have a more doubtful claim.

the merits both of the middle-range ideas and of the implicit more general theoretical positions; we shall then go on to discuss the use they make of others' theorising, and the nature of their general theoretical style.

The assumptions I shall make in this discussion are that the role of theory is to enable the theoriser to explain, understand and predict phenomena that he is interested in. It does this by providing propositions which have been established with a reasonable degree of confidence about the causal relationships which hold within populations of defined scope, and by suggesting ones which have not yet been established or whose scope has not yet been explored. Any explanatory or predictive statement implies some such generalising proposition(s), even if they are not stated as such. A good sociological explanation or prediction is one that is not merely logically adequate to account for the phenomena concerned, but also adequate 'on the level of meaning': that is, it can explain why men to whom situations and their own actions have meanings should act in that way rather than another when in that situation.[4] It will thus, when fully stated, contain references both to external factors and to the interpretations made of them.* (When a theoretical statement does not contain both it may be either because something was taken for granted and so not mentioned, or because for some reason it is a genuinely incomplete explanation.)

Theorising about the Family

The subject on which the most connected theoretical ideas are stated in the Institute's opus is that of the family, and in particular the working-class family as found in Bethnal Green. The major ideas are stated in the first two books, and several later ones touch on the same or related themes. To a greater or lesser degree these themes are scattered through the books; we shall attempt to state them here in a unified way, which in this case can be done without falsification since the books are intentionally related.

* All this is stated dogmatically, although I am aware that there is scope for disagreement, because this does not seem the appropriate place to go into familiar arguments on a subject where my position is not an original one. The references suggest starting places for anyone not yet familiar with them who wishes to read on the subject.

100

The theorising about the family starts from the observation of certain patterns which are felt to need accounting for. Townsend and Young and Willmott give a picture of the family system of Bethnal Green as one characterised by the prevalence of extended families* of three or more generations, matrilocality, a particularly strong mother—daughter tie, and segregation of conjugal roles. This system revolves primarily around the women, and the men who have connections with two sets of women tend to restrict their contacts with their wives' relatives, especially their mothers. Women's lives are seen as bound up with home and relatives, while men have social relationships based more on work and friends made outside the home; for both sexes, however, wide groups of kin provide links to other groupings in the community. Townsend in addition found that forms of substitution seemed to take place by which if appropriate relatives were missing someone else was frequently as it were co-opted to play their roles. More or less clear and explicit explanations have been suggested for each of these features, and the explanations are of course interrelated.

The prevalence of 'extended' families is accounted for partly by factors to some extent specific to Bethnal Green, which are seen as facilitating it, partly by historical circumstances true of the working class in general, which are seen as having created needs which an extended family can satisfy, and partly by demographic reasons.

The density of housing and long residence of most people in Bethnal Green facilitate the establishment of stable relationships with other family members living nearby, and it is possible to stay in close proximity because landlords are prepared to allocate houses to relatives of other tenants, and because a sufficient variety of jobs is available locally to make it rare for young people to need to move in search of work to suit their tastes.[5] The positive reasons for the extended family pattern, as opposed to those which merely facilitate it, are seen in the historical insecurity of working-class women at earlier stages of industrialisation. Husbands

* The working definition of an extended family is any case where members of two or more nuclear families live together, or live close to each other and share household tasks and spend a lot of time together ('Family and Kinship in East London', pp. 202-3).

101

often died young, leaving them and their children without support; when alive they were often unemployed, and so could only offer weak support; and even when employed they often kept their families short of money.[6] The extended family was the women's trade union, providing economic and moral support and help in caring for children. Finally, the demographic reasons adduced: firstly, socially defined childhood ends young in Bethnal Green, when the adolescent leaves school and goes out to work, so that by the time young people marry they have had their fling of independence and are ready to take up ties with their parents once more;[7] secondly, the usual pattern (at least in the past) of early marriage and long childbearing means that there is little or no gap for a couple between the end of a period when they are rearing their own children, and the beginning of the period when they can help with grandchildren and are coming to need help in infirmity themselves.[8] Both these reasons tend to create generational continuity.

Obviously the historical reasons outlined above also help to explain why the tie between mother and daughter should be such a strong one, but there is a further argument on this point. This is that women have the bond of the shared work of housekeeping and childrearing, which both gives them a common interest and means that it is mutually convenient for them to help each other. In a way this bond could exist between any two married women, related or not, but it is more likely to be effective when they have shared their previous lives and know each other's ways.[9] When it was found that the mother—daughter tie remained particularly strong even in Woodford, Young and Willmott became convinced that the factor of shared interests alone was sufficient to account for it, irrespective of class. It would follow that where father and son work together at the same job their ties should be as close as the women's, and this is indeed argued.[10] * On the same basis the finding that social mobility seemed to affect the contacts of sons with fathers more than those of daughters with mothers is explained by

* It is not, however, studied systematically. Figures are given for the proportion of husbands in the marriage sample having the same occupations as their fathers, but not on how many of them actually work with relatives, which need not correlate much; it would be theoretically valuable to be able to distinguish between the effects of constant interaction and of shared interests.

102

saying that jobs (which define the 'classes' between which mobility has taken place) are more salient for men than for women, who retain the same central occupation whatever their husbands may do.[11] The tendency to matrilocality follows from the general existence and recognition of this special bond.

The segregation of conjugal roles — that is, the leading by husband and wife of rather separate social lives, and the rigid division of household tasks into men's and (more often) women's work — is explained in a slightly different way. It bulks larger in Townsend's descriptions than in Young and Willmott's, no doubt chiefly because he focuses on the elderly, while Young and Willmott are concerned with younger generations and maintain that role-segregation has decreased markedly even within living memory.[12] Townsend explains it as a consequence of the couple's commitments to their own extended families: 'The maintenance of separate loyalties outside the marriage is a possible source of continuous friction between man and wife. Such friction is reduced or avoided by . . . a fairly strict division of labour and of income and by segregation in associations with relatives and others.'[13] Young and Willmott's suggestion that the mother—daughter tie is less important in Woodford, though still strong, because the husband—wife tie there is stronger,[14] can supplement this, though there are some difficulties, which we shall discuss later, in reconciling the two sets of underlying assumptions. The reasons Young and Willmott offer in their earlier book for decreasing degrees of segregation are multiple: the birth-rate has fallen, which means that women are emancipated from childrearing and can achieve some independence by going out to work, so husbands recognise more responsibilities in the home; the death-rate has fallen, giving greater financial and emotional security to women; housing has improved, making their homes relatively more attractive to men; working hours have decreased, so that they have more time to spend in their homes; and ideas move more freely through the mass media, putting new models of behaviour from the wider society before Bethnal Greeners.[15] Presumably to the extent that Bethnal Green still differs from other areas along these dimensions it is to be expected that conjugal roles will still be more segregated there.

Finally, the tendency for men to have only limited contacts with their wives' relatives, and to be particularly reserved with their mothers-in-law, is explained as a way of resolving the strain created by potentially conflicting claims of husband and mother over their wife and daughter; the secondary tendency for the husband to be drawn into the sphere of his wife's mother rather than staying in that of his own extended family of origin is, similarly, seen as a use of the principle of female dominance in the kinship network to resolve the tension between the claims of their two mothers over the couple.

All these explanations may be considered at two levels: in terms of their adequacy to account for the particular concrete phenomena, and in terms of the more fundamental theoretical models that they imply. These two levels are of course related, but the distinction is a convenient one. The theoretical position implied by some of the arguments is a functionalist one, where particular practices are argued to exist because they perform functions that tend to maintain a system in equilibrium. There are considerable logical difficulties about the explanatory adequacy of this position,[17] but since it is not formally stated as such I shall treat these only insofar as they arise in specific contexts.

Before going on to discuss the merits of the specific arguments, it will be useful to fill in a bit more the sense in which the family patterns of Bethnal Green are treated as constituting a system. The most obvious sense in which this is so is that its different parts are seen to fit together into a consistent and coherent whole, which is capable of perpetuating itself from one generation to the next: conjugal role-segregation is encouraged by the strength of a new couple's ties to their extended families, and in its turn creates a need for practical and moral support from others besides the spouse; large numbers of children make a wife's need for help when they are young greater, and also make it less of a burden for this help to be repaid when they are grown up and the older generation who have given it are themselves in need . . . and so on. Townsend also sees it as a system in the sense that where there is any disturbance to the normative pattern, for instance through the death or non-existence of the suitable relative to play the key role, there are mechanisms of substi-

104

tution which come into play to produce an approximation to it: '... the extended family of three generations is a self-balancing or self-correcting institution to which the principles of *replacement* and *compensation* are fundamental.'[18] Young and Willmott say almost nothing about variations on the basic pattern, so this theme is not stressed in their books. They, however, seem to regard the family less as an autonomous system and more as one that is inextricably involved with economic conditions; this idea is taken up and developed much more strongly by Peter Marris when he studies conditions in Lagos and makes comparisons with Bethnal Green.[19] (Townsend's relative neglect of economic factors can perhaps be attributed to the fact that his subjects were old people, most of whom had retired from work.) In all the books the idea of reciprocity of services given and received as the basis of solidarity between generations is stressed, and so norms which prescribe the giving of services are seen as functional for the system.

We return now to consider the particular explanations suggested, treating them as far as possible in the order in which they have been outlined above. First, therefore, we shall discuss the reasons given for the prevalence of the extended family.

The distinction between positive and merely facilitating reasons is one between those which make the extended family system functional and those which make it possible. In the list of those which make it possible the only one worth querying is the point about the variety of jobs available locally; as the authors themselves point out, in times of less than full employment the advantages of sponsorship by relatives make *lack* of variety give greater support to family ties, and a shared job provides another basis of solidarity.

The supposed functionality of the extended family as the women's trade union, at least in part, raises several issues. First, as the authors again point out,[20] too strong an attachment between women and their mothers might itself produce the effect, which supposedly it was defending them against, of driving their husbands out. To the extent that this was so it could be described as functional in the sense that it tended to perpetuate the same pattern, but not in the sense that it provided the optimal solution to a problem. Thus this could

105

be seen as a natural line of behaviour for women individually faced with certain problems, though not one that tended to solve them for the system as a whole. Further, it is not very convincingly argued that the extended family would be functional chiefly for the women; presumably they too died young, leaving the children on their husbands' hands, and men at that time more often got help from relatives in their work. Finally, two more radical points can be made. Other sets of arrangements might have been able to perform the same functions, and that which was functional in past circumstances is not likely to be so in the present if circumstances have changed; to explain why one particular solution was arrived at, and why it persists despite apparent dysfunctions, is hard without the introduction of the concept of *norms* which distinguish some solutions as inherently more desirable to the participants than others. To suggest that norms have developed which positively favour such patterns of family behaviour is to provide an explanation which is both logically more watertight (since it accounts for the growth of one set of potentially functional arrangements rather than another) and more adequate on the level of meaning (since it indicates why people should choose consciously to act as they do). Such an explanation in terms of norms is of a basically different kind from a functionalist one, if the latter is more than tautological — which is what it becomes when any behaviour that conforms to norms is *ipso facto* defined as functional for the system. Functional explanations are again tautological if they explain x only by pointing out that it is functional for y, and y by its functionality for x; this seems to be what is being done for conjugal role-segregation and the extended family, unless an independent original cause for one of them is also suggested.* It is not clear that a satisfactory original cause has in this case been proposed. It may be easier to account for the extended family if this issue is kept separate from that of the special links among women.

* As R. P. Dore points out, this type of analysis can plausibly be applied to the cause of the *persistence* of a given institutional pattern, but not to the cause of its *origin* (Ronald Philip Dore, 'Function and Cause', in 'American Sociological Review', xxvi 6 (Dec 1961) 843-53). Two institutions already in existence may be mutually reinforcing, but that does not explain how they got there in the first place.

But before passing on to treat this we must briefly deal with the demographic reasons advanced for the extended family pattern. The argument about the relatively early end to working-class social childhood is rather odd, because middle-class children marry later as well as achieving other forms of independence later; this means that the length of the period between the establishment of independence and marriage may well be much the same, in which case the stronger ties after marriage between working-class children and their parents remain unaccounted for. The argument about early marriage and late childbearing 'explains' why working-class couples should spend longer proportions of their life spans closely involved in relationships spanning the generations, in the trivial sense that they are then bound to spend longer in rearing their children, but does not explain at all why they should help any particular child with the grand-children or receive help in turn. The need is explained, but not why it should be met, and in this way; to explain that, norms, or some other factor, need to be introduced.

What about the strength of the tie between mother and daughter? There are no obvious objections to be made to the explanations offered for this, since they seem adequate to account for it even without the introduction of functionalist ideas. But at least one other explanation could be suggested which seems *equally* adequate, and this is one that attributes the tie to the mother's predominant role in socialising the children, plus the fact that male children are not expected to, and in later life hardly could, use her as a role-model. A choice between such plausible *a priori* alternatives can only be made on the basis of the support they receive from empirical evidence, and Young and Willmott have not pro-vided evidence appropriate for this purpose.[21] Such evidence might also have helped to bring about a more precise specifi-cation of the processes by which such a close tie is supposed to be established, and this would have been useful for predic-tion to new situations. Might it be, for instance, that the deviant cases in which women do *not* have a close tie with their mothers could be accounted for by differences in their occupational situations?

There is some obscurity about what is supposed to have happened in Woodford: the mother—daughter tie is still strong

— but proportionately less important as the husband—wife one is more so, and moreover it is to some extent replaced by relationships with other, unrelated women with whom the same sorts of services are exchanged.[22] If socialisation were crucial, only Mum would do; if the exchange of services were crucial, almost any other willing married woman with children would do. If Mum is highly accessible, she meets both criteria; but to be prepared to move away from her, when there is any real choice in the matter, suggests that the attachment to her is already relatively weak or normatively weakly supported. These considerations imply, once again, that norms may be relevant — norms both about behaviour within the family, and about the relative weight to be attached to family and other ties and pressures.

It has been suggested that a strong mother—daughter tie is in some ways an alternative to a strong husband—wife one; now we consider the relationship of husband and wife directly. Townsend's explanation for the segregation of conjugal roles, quoted above, falls into some of the classic difficulties of functionalist statements. Firstly, it talks about the positive functions of segregation without considering whether it may not have counterbalancing dysfunctions; if it has, as can plausibly be argued,[23] an explanation in terms of functions is logically inadequate — if functionality were intrinsically causal, some better net balance of functions and dysfunctions would have come about. Secondly, it regards conjugal relationships as functionally adapting themselves to the couples' existing commitments to their extended families, but gives no clue why it should be the conjugal relationships that adapt to the family commitments rather than vice versa. Thus the argument as stated does not sound very plausible, although a detailed expansion of it could certainly make it sound more so.

Rather than attempt such an expansion I shall suggest instead the introduction of non-functionalist ideas, which are needed in any case to suggest how functions may in practice be translated into causes. Thus we may suggest, as Bott does,[24] that extended family commitments take priority over ties between husband and wife quite simply because they come first in time. The next question is why the new marriage tie does not radically change the situation, and

108

Bott's answer is that it does when the new couple's social network is loose-knit, which tends to come about whenever they and the other members of the network are physically mobile. Townsend is aware of Bott's theory, and says in a footnote[25] that he wants to lay more stress on the couple's membership of close-knit three-generation *family* groups than on the connectedness of their whole social networks; he doesn't explain why, so we must speculate as we compare his argument with Bott's.

Bott's argument becomes more complex when it is looked at in more detail, and we see why she thinks a close-knit network should have these effects. She suggests that a close-knit network tends to reach a consensus on norms and so exert consistent pressures on its members to conform to them, and to keep in touch with and help each other; when spouses come to their marriage already members of such networks they will not need to get so much of their emotional satisfaction, or practical help, from each other. The relationship between the connectedness of the network and consensus on norms is obvious, but it is not at all obvious why connectedness — as opposed to simple numbers of members in each spouse's social circle — should affect the availability of aid or social contacts and emotional support. This only follows if the *content* of the norms on which there is a consensus is specified, and indeed later comments make it clear that Bott realises that this is a crucial variable. She notes that in areas where close-knit networks are typical there are norms which limit legitimate heterosexual associations to kin, so that husband and wife come to their marriage with already established habits of associating with their own sexes; in her description of couples with loose-knit networks, on the other hand, she specifies a norm by which loyalties to the spouse take priority over other kin loyalties.[26] If the weight of consensus in the network backs up such norms, whatever their content, they are clearly likely to have a strong influence on the couple; if the network is loose-knit, couples will be thrown back more on their own resources* in working out a viable pattern for their marriage. Thus there is a stronger

* Or perhaps on reference groups distinct from their immediate social networks, and here norms are again likely to come in as determinants of the choice of reference group. At this point the rather fundamental question of the genesis of norms might be raised.

element of subculture in Bott's explanation than at first appears. (If this is not regarded as a fair statement of *her* views, I would maintain that it is a necessary modification of them.)

How does Townsend's stress on the close-knit three-generation family instead of the whole network compare with this? Presumably his argument would be that husband and wife come to their marriage embedded in different family networks — and stay in them. But this runs up against the same sort of problem as the first statement of Bott's argument: if the connectedness is important, it must be because it implies the enforcement of shared norms, whose content needs to be specified and here must advocate segregation. If, on the other hand, the emphasis is not particularly on the connectedness of the family network, the explanation seems to be simply one in terms of habit; one then needs to explain why the partners in middle-class marriages do not stay embedded in their families of origin. In either case it seems to amount simply to saying that the system continues because the system continues, or that there is a subculture which is causally autonomous. This is not really an explanation, nor does it seem consistent with an approach which sees some aspects of the family system as responses to (past) economic circumstances; if a broader social context was relevant once, it may be so again.

Young and Willmott certainly treat this broader context as relevant, though not in any very coherent way; most of their suggested reasons for decreasing segregation are not very convincing. Working-class housing has improved, but haven't the pubs too? and anyway some of the inhabitants of Bethnal Green are still living in the same old housing; are their conjugal roles noticeably different from those of the couples in new council flats? Working hours have decreased, but that could mean more time free to spend at the pub rather than at home. The birth-rate has fallen, but the causes of this are so implicated with conjugal roles that one cannot simply treat it as a cause of changes in them;[27] it might also be an effect. The mass media present alternative models of behaviour, but would these be followed if Bethnal Greeners did not already hold values that made them seem attractive?

If we ignore those rather casually made suggestions, we are

110

left with the more developed idea that the husband—wife tie is a casualty of the mother—daughter one. The sense in which the two could be alternatives is not very carefully worked out, but there seem to be two possibilities: (i) time is limited, so the more spent with one person the less there is to spend with another; (ii) emotional needs or resources are limited, so the more are satisfied by or spent on one person the less there is for another. Both these possibilities could only explain why one tie should be stronger than another if the intensity of the first tie was already given, and took up more than half of the available time or emotion. The second also makes the rather dubious assumption that emotional needs and resources are somehow homogeneous; aprioristically the alternative assumption that they can be diverse, and different ones can be better satisfied by different people, sounds at least equally plausible. But this is psychological rather than sociological reasoning.

This discussion could be carried further, but it is in danger of becoming speculative for lack of material to work on; most of the theoretical statements made by the Institute on these issues have been too brief and imprecise for more detailed exegesis and comment to be profitable. Certain basic problems in sociological explanation are raised by the ideas put forward, but it is not clear whether these ideas are supported by a conscious and consistent underlying theoretical position implying answers to the problems; the lack of explicit justification suggests that they may instead be *ad hoc* responses to particular substantive issues as they arise.

The one comment that can confidently be made is that the natures of the mechanisms supposed to connect cause and effect have not usually been as carefully stated as might be wished. This must be at least in part ascribed to the descriptive intent of many of the books, which has meant that hypotheses have not been formulated in advance and data have therefore only fortuitously been collected about such mechanisms. It is odd that one factor in the process of causation that is often missing should be the norms and values of those involved, since this plays a major role in their discussion of class, which we consider next. Perhaps the authors' own values make them more willing to see working-class family patterns than they are to see other characteristics of

111

the working class, or its general position in society, as functional.

Theorising about Class

'Class' is the other major subject of theorising by members of the Institute; it appears mainly as an independent variable, although there are some ambiguities about its status which are discussed below. We shall start our consideration of the way in which it is used by outlining the description of British class structure conveyed through the Institute's works. This description is in terms of working- and middle-class ways of life and value systems.

The working-class way of life is seen as involving the extended family embedded in a stable and predominantly working-class community with great neighbourliness and communal solidarity, expressed in networks of social relations and mutual aid and strong attachment to the local area and its primary groups. In this context people are known and judged as individuals with multiple characteristics rather than as the holders of certain jobs or owners of certain possessions. Because they are known so well, and because of the basic economic homogeneity of the area, pretensions to higher status get little credit and are rarely made; anyone who seriously aspires to other standards is liable to leave the community. Labour sympathies are taken for granted, though there are few formal organisational affiliations, and economic advancement is achieved collectively through trade unionism. Children leave school as early as possible, and go into manual jobs which are often found through family contacts.[28] In adolescence they go around in groups and have relatively little involvement in the extended family, but when (probably in their late teens) the stage of serious courtship is reached they re-enter the kin network. In childhood and adolescence minor delinquency is common, at least among boys, but more serious offences are confined to a small minority and disapproved by the adult community.

The value system seen as underpinning these behaviour patterns has as its key themes those of collectivism and the labour theory of value.[29] Collectivism is shown by 'the ethic

112

of reciprocity' in mutual aid within the family and local community, maintained by continuous contacts over long periods of time, and by the solidarity of all these overlapping groups against such middle-class outsiders as the police and the schools. These are defined as outsiders not merely because they are relatively unfamiliar but also because they are threatening to the self-respect of the community; this is where the 'labour theory of value' comes in. This evaluates the worth of jobs, and thus of the people doing them, by the direct contribution they make to the production of obviously useful goods; on this criterion almost all manual jobs are defined as superior to almost all non-manual jobs, giving a reversal of the common status-order. It follows from this that education, particularly of a non-vocational kind, is not highly valued, since it keeps children out of useful work in the short run without leaving them any better qualified for it. It also follows that there are strong sanctions against competitiveness or striving for different standards, since these breach community solidarity or imply preferences for other ways of life; the middle-class 'Protestant ethic' thus gets no sympathy, and this lack of sympathy is encouraged by the short-run perspective and consequent inability (or lack of desire) to defer gratifications created by the typical modes of payment and conditions of service of manual workers.

The middle-class pattern of life counterposed to this is one where nuclear families move freely about the country in pursuit of career advantages, and individually chosen friends take the place of neighbours and extended family. Mutual aid is less necessary and so less prevalent, though elderly parents are looked after and unrelated wives exchange services. There are more formal organisational memberships, and more highly developed social skills in the achievement of new relationships. Middle-class living areas are not to the same extent living communities, and the more superficial knowledge which their more transient inhabitants have of each other leads to judgements being made in terms of status and possessions. These are seen, however, as legitimate objects of aspiration, to be pursued by deliberate policies; educational and occupational aspirations are high, and advancement is achieved by individual effort and sacrifice.

The middle-class value system is seen as being one which

113

sets great store by material possessions, advocates continual striving to improve one's position in life even at the cost of sacrificing present gratifications, and attaches importance to status as acquired through superior educational standards, position in occupational hierarchies, and possessions. These values entail less dominant concern for personal relationships with particular people, and greater social isolation of the nuclear family, though this may not at all mean that middle-class couples have or prefer fewer social contacts.

The main features of the working-class culture described are explained by the traditional insecurity, low earnings and low status of manual workers. Insecurity and low earnings create a special need for mutual support in adversity; the absence of opportunities for promotion or individual economic advancement allows long residence in one area, and encourages group identification for collective advancement. The solidarity this creates is inconsistent with individual striving to get ahead, so both community social controls and lack of local opportunity encourage migration by those who want to do this. Local solidarity is also encouraged by low status in the wider community, which creates a need for psychological defences (the labour theory of value) which can most effectively be maintained when contacts with other groups are minimised. The homogeneity of a one-class area makes social controls consistent and thus very effective. Attachment to the local area is encouraged not only by length of residence and communal solidarity but also by the consequent dense network of highly localised social relationships, and its circular effect in depriving inhabitants of the chance to develop the social skills used in less ascriptive contacts.

There is again a strong functionalist element in this line of explanation: practices are explained by being shown to meet a need. What is not really explained — and this is a common defect of functionalist explanations — is the nature of the process by which the need comes to be met; there is no reason to assume that a benevolent providence ensures that needs are met automatically.

There are two major alternative ways of explaining why needs in general should be met. The first simply says that people concerned perceive the need, and therefore take

114

deliberate steps to meet it; this obviously happens in some cases, but provides a very implausible account in many others where there is no evidence that a practice was so purposefully instituted. In this case, for example, trade unions seem to fit the model much better than does the extended family.

The second possibility is that in the long run needs come to be met by existing institutions simply because those which don't meet them, however they came into existence in the first place, are less likely to survive; they are found inadequate and abandoned, or the people using them are less successful and therefore become of decreasing social importance if they don't actually die out. This seems much more plausible; but it means that of the practices found at any one time some may be mainly dysfunctional, even if for that reason declining, so that their present existence cannot be explained by their functionality. It is often hard to demonstrate empirically that such an evolutionary process has taken place, and even if it has this leaves unexplained the origin of the practices which then do or do not survive. A more serious difficulty is that fitness to survive is specific to a given environment; if a dysfunctional practice can get as far as starting, it becomes part of the environment, and rather than it changing other aspects may change to suit it; the theory then becomes simply one of a long-run strain towards institutional consistency. This may be a valid theory, but if the concept of 'need' becomes so relativistic it loses all meaning.

If we accept that neither of these two ways of explaining why needs should invariably be met is satisfactory, it cannot be assumed that needs have a general propensity to be met. This means that the meeting of needs has to be explained *ad hoc* in particular cases, which in this area the Institute have often not done. A case where they have, which may serve as an example of a more satisfactory style of explanation, is the use made of the variable of long residence in the area. This can itself be accounted for partly by the age of the housing and partly by other social factors (for which see above), and without the introduction of the concept of need can plausibly go some way towards explaining communal solidarity, which in turn is likely to reinforce the tendency to long residence by making inhabitants reluctant to move elsewhere.

A case where the functionalist type of explanation stands alone is that where they relate insecurity to mutual support. The two may be causally related, but for them to appear convincingly so the intervening variables must be specified which lead from problem to solution. Thus the argument here is not that the connections made by the Institute are wrong, so much as that the reasoning is incomplete; only if it were spelt out in more detail could the validity of the theoretical propositions be discussed.

So far we have been considering the broad descriptions given of the patterns treated as typical of working and middle class; some exceptions to these patterns do, however, appear in the books, mainly in the form of upward mobility (never downward) and atypical aspirations. Some working-class parents, particularly mothers, were keen on education for their children and encouraged them through grammar school.[30] Some working-class children get white collar-jobs, and/or aspire to better material conditions than Bethnal Green or Dagenham provide physically or support socially; they move to other areas and ways of life.[31] Such a move seldom means that relations with close kin are broken off, though there are some complaints of snobbism, but greater physical distance inevitably creates barriers to interaction even if cars and telephones help to break them down.[32] People with manual jobs in predominantly middle-class communities do not move to escape, but their traditional way of life is under some pressure from the social environment; some of them react by maintaining the traditional patterns as far as possible, but others attempt to adopt the middle-class patterns.

This last point is one of several which suggest that there may be some differentiation in attitudes and styles of life even within the working class, but this theme is never developed; there are slightly more explicit references to differentiation within the middle class, but again not developed. The broad and ideal-typical nature of the main descriptions creates a number of problems, which will be discussed shortly. Before this, we shall consider the explanations offered for the occurrence of non-traditional behaviour, which the reasons given so far cannot account for. To be consistent, these should argue that where non-traditional

116

behaviour takes place some circumstance held to cause the traditional pattern is absent or some new circumstance is present.

Most of the explanations given exactly fit this model. Thus the relative absence of communal solidarity and neighbourliness is explained by the shortness of residence typical of a new or middle-class housing area; a competitive emphasis on status is explained by the lack of detailed personal knowledge about each other that residents on a new estate have;[34] this lack of knowledge is explained not only by the newness of the estate but also by the lack of social skills for striking up friendships among people who come from long-established areas like Bethnal Green;[35] the departure by many working-class inhabitants of Woodford from the norms of Bethnal Green is explained by the predominantly middle-class character of the area, which means that other models of behaviour are available and have high status and are favoured by what community controls there are.[36] These explanations are as adequate as the general ones from which they are derived, discussed above. Perhaps also in this category is the suggestion that women at Greenleigh become snobbish and concerned with status because their new houses are much superior to the old ones, and a woman's status is tied up with that of her house as a man's is with that of his job.[37] But this cannot on its own account for snobbishness in relation to other people in identical houses; some sort of reference group idea is also implied.

More striking than the explanations given, however, is the absence of explanation at certain key points. Instances of deviance or differences which go unexplained are: the existence of people who get white-collar jobs and/or aspire to move elsewhere and achieve higher material standards in Bethnal Green and Dagenham; the division of working-class people in Woodford into those whose lives follow the patterns of Bethnal Green and of the Woodford middle class; and the division of adolescent boys in Bethnal Green into 'real' and merely developmental delinquents, and into the 'working-class', 'middle-class' and 'rebel' types in the typology given. (Perhaps the manual workers in Woodford who call themselves middle-class may also be mentioned here. Their 'mis'-identification is accounted for by their similarity

117

in consumption standards to the occupationally middle-class,[38] but since there is no evidence which came first this amounts to a non-explanation.)

If such deviant cases or diverse reactions can occur under what appears to be the same circumstances as those of the non-deviant ones, neither set of circumstances can have been investigated in enough detail to account adequately for the outcomes; thus if deviant cases are left unexplained the explanations given for the non-deviant also become questionable. The admitted existence of such cases tends to suggest that the account given of working-class life is too broad and stereotyped to apply to the working class as a whole, even if it applies to some sections; this suggestion is supported by the absence of any more than passing mention of the distinction between 'rough' and 'respectable' found by other researchers, or of the 'deferential' social type. [39] To describe one particular pattern as though it were *the* working-class way of life, and other patterns were departures from it to be accounted for by special factors, is to imply that the factors in the first case are somehow inherently or typically working-class, while the others are exceptional. It is not at all evident that such an implication about the patterns found in Bethnal Green could be justified, and even if it could this justification has not been given.

This tendency to stereotypy probably stems in part from the use of highly localised samples which are liable to be dominated by one class, and thus make rather broad statements seem relatively plausible. This also supports the propensity to describe one class by contrast or antithesis with another. The heuristic usefulness of constructing contrasted types is obvious, but the procedure can have unfortunate consequences.[40] If a class (or any other group) is described by the respects in which it differs from another, more significant characteristics which they have in common may be neglected, and so differences between classes get a false emphasis. If a class is described by the characteristics of a majority of its members, large minorities with equal claim to membership may be set on one side and so differences within classes will be underplayed. In either case the resultant description is to some extent a distortion of the evidence.[41] The Institute has tended to fall into this trap.

118

In fact it is not at all clear how empirically prevalent the values described as typically working-class are, since no direct evidence on this is provided; the complete set *might* be held by no one, or only by the elderly or some other minority. (And to the extent that they are held it might be pragmatically, rather than with a normative commitment to them as autotelic, so that other values would become apparent if circumstances changed; this sort of process is suggested by Peter Marris's discussions of the relations between economic factors and patterns of family life.[42]) The article on 'Social Grading by Manual Workers', for instance, on whose data most of the ideas about the labour theory of value are based, shows that only 22 out of the sample of 82 manual workers deviated consistently from the Hall-Jones scale's prestige ranking of occupations, and that these were on average slightly less skilled than the remainder. 'Family and Class in a London Suburb' argues that club membership and visiting among friends are especially middle-class. But the figures given show that nearly half of the middle-class group (as compared with two-thirds of the working-class one) do not belong to any club, and that the largest percentage difference between classes in the recency with which they have had a visit from a friend or neighbour is eleven per cent (pp. 91, 109). Differences of this order, even if statistically 'significant', hardly justify the use made of them. Though the Institute is by no means alone in the tendency to do this — indeed it seems almost universal in contemporary sociology — it does become especially pernicious when so little clue is given to the size and distinguishing characteristics of minority groups.

Closely related to this tendency is the way in which the distinction between the characteristics of the members of a class, and of an area in which that class is in a majority, is blurred; this is particularly marked in the comparisons made between Woodford and Bethnal Green.[43] Minorities can only legitimately be passed over in this way when the grouping within which they constitute a minority can be regarded as a real sociological whole or unit. If Woodford is a distinct and integrated community, it makes sense to talk about it as a whole; if the working class (as defined by occupation) is a coherent social group, it makes sense to attribute its group-

E

level characteristics even to individual members who do not possess them at the individual level. Whether or not these are the case is a matter for empirical research which has not yet been done. They certainly cannot be assumed, but this assumption often comes about as an accidental by-product of the research procedure. If, for instance, the researcher breaks his sample down into 'working-class' and 'middle-class' respondents, it is a small verbal step from the convenience of referring to these categories by the names given them to their reification, by treating the words as though they were *known* to refer to meaningful entities 'out there' rather than having been created by the researcher. Of course there may well be such meaningful entities, but their existence needs to be demonstrated.

This leads us to consider how far the Institute regard 'classes' as real entities, and more generally what the meaning is that they attribute to the term 'class'. This is nowhere directly stated, so it will have to be inferred from the statements that are made. A good place to start is the operational definitions of it used in the various research projects.

Firstly, the operational definition given to class is always one based on occupation; respondents in the surveys are normally classified as 'working-class' or 'middle-class' according to whether their occupation (or in the case of married women their husband's occupation) is classified as manual or non-manual. Some modified version of the Registrar-General's classification of occupations is used for this. From these facts alone it is not evident what the basis of division is assumed to be. 'Manual' and 'non-manual' sound like categories based on the inherent nature of the task performed, but examination of the jobs classified as one or the other throws doubt on this; why, to use a standard example, should a printer count as 'manual' but a copy-typist as 'non-manual'? Obviously social criteria are also being used, and they relate to status rather than to class in the strict sense.

The same sort of classification is also commonly used when occupational status is the underlying criterion, and this enters into the Registrar-General's version. The basic classification is in fact so highly conventionalised that to understand what particular meanings are given to it by the Institute it is more instructive to look at the modifications and com-

120

ments made on it. This gives us two instances where style of life seems to be the criterion used: marginal cases are classified on the basis of their general (unspecified) similarity to 'manual' workers whose jobs are not regarded as marginal,[44] and it is remarked that many of the 'non-manual' workers in Bethnal Green are shopkeepers and publicans who really resemble working-class people more than they do the administrators and professionals with whom they are classified.[45]

There are also at least three further instances where references are made to the internal differentiation of the two basic 'classes'. In the introduction to 'Family and Class in a London Suburb' it is stated that in Woodford the 'upper' or 'upper-middle' class is absent, and that people there in occupations that might be thought to place them in this higher bracket in fact led lives very similar to those of the rest of the (middle- or lower- ?) 'middle' class (p. xii). Then in 'Adolescent Boys of East London' the manual group is several times divided into 'skilled' and 'semi-skilled and unskilled', but no particular rationale is offered for this, though there are shown to be differences between these sub-groups (pp. 75, 98, 103, 115). The contexts in which the distinction appears suggest that when the boys' own work is being discussed the emphasis is literally on the nature of the work done, while when their education is being related to their fathers' work the emphasis is in a vaguer way on 'class' as it determines opportunities and the uses made of them. Lastly, in 'The Evolution of a Community' the occupational structure is broken down into five groups: 'professional and managerial', 'clerical and shop workers', and 'skilled', 'semi-skilled' and 'unskilled' manual. This detailed division is not used subsequently in the book, where all the manual are lumped together as 'working-class', those on the estate with non-manual jobs are called 'white-collar', and those off the estate in professional or managerial jobs are called 'middle-class' (pp. 14-15).* This again suggests a distinction between those who are and aren't *really* 'middle-class', with the basis

* The original text is ambiguously worded, so that it is not clear whether living on the estate is regarded as disqualifying from the 'middle class' or whether it merely happens to be the case that none of them do live there. I assume the latter is meant.

of the distinction again not specified.

In several of the books the occupational division is presented with comments which show that it is not occupation as such which is the key to the authors' concept of 'class'. 'Family and Class in a London Suburb' says:

> There are many possible criteria of social class — family connexions, education, occupation, accent, income, power, property. ... our society is fluid enough so that these attributes are not necessarily matched. ... This means that no single index is entirely satisfactory, though some are better than others. (p. xi)

A very similar statement is made in 'The Evolution of a Community', to the effect that occupation is only one of a number of possible criteria, and Willmott goes on to add that '... one of the key questions is how far the people at Dagenham are what is thought of as 'working-class' in other ways — in their social behaviour, in their attitudes, and so on (p. 51). The only clue given to what *is* 'thought of' as working-class comes later on, when it is concluded that Dagenham is still 'predominantly working-class ... in sentiment' (p. 108); this conclusion is reached at the end of a chapter which shows that despite improved standards of living most people there voted Labour, identified themselves as working-class when asked, and showed few signs of status striving over possessions. Finally, 'Family and Kinship in East London' uses a slightly different implicit definition of the foundations of a shared life-style when it points out that similar jobs entail similarities in formal education, working conditions, membership of trade unions and Labour Party support (p. 72). ('Entail', obviously, carries several meanings here.)

Thus cumulatively it becomes evident that the operational definition in terms of occupational status is only meant as an indicator of a whole style of life; some of the components of such styles are sketched in. It is exceedingly difficult to find any simple and direct measure of styles of life, not merely empirically but in principle, because by definition they consist of complex sets of characteristics which may not appear in finite and mutually exclusive combinations. (But only to the extent that they do, and that the number of

122

combinations is fairly small, can the concept legitimately be used in social research.) It must be this technical problem which has led the members of the Institute to persist, along with many other social researchers, in basing their operational definition of class on a crude classification of occupations even when it is clear that this does not indicate what they really have in mind.

This procedure has practical convenience, but also the great weakness that it forces the researcher back on what everyone 'knows'. The conventional occupational divisions correlate roughly with what everyone 'knows' to be class boundaries, and so the nature of these boundaries and the extent to which the occupational divisions correlate with them in sociologically meaningful ways are not investigated. This becomes particularly unfortunate when the data collected on this basis are used to make generalisations about the characteristics of classes and the consequences of belonging to them, since it's not clear what the units are to which such generalisations are supposed to apply.

While this problem remains unresolved, and the distinguishing features of particular styles of life have not been isolated and defined, it is not clear which aspects of the observed patterns are to be regarded as crucial and which as merely their correlates. Until this decision has been made, any concept of class as style of life is likely to remain so broad that it cannot be used in theoretical statements as either an independent or a dependent variable; this is because it already includes, or can easily be stretched to include, almost anything that might be correlated with a concept of more precise and limited scope.

This danger may be illustrated by some examples. In 'Family and Class in a London Suburb' the conclusion that class is a 'decisive' influence on family life (p. 86) comes at the end of a chapter in which it is shown that even in Woodford 'working-class' people live nearer to their relatives and see more of them than do 'middle-class' people. A careful reading of the chapter shows no stated reasons why this should be so, except the negative one implied by citing instances where status considerations have set social barriers between them and upwardly mobile relatives; an earlier chapter (ch. iii) suggests that different classes have different

123

preferences, and that middle-class career mobility intensifies their effects. Distinctively middle-class modes of contact with relatives are accounted for by a greater ability to write letters, and by their having (the money to afford) spare rooms, cars and telephones. But any of these variables — possessions, income, education, career patterns, values — could and sometimes does serve as part of a *definition* of class, as much as something that explains why classes differ. The same could be said about educational aspirations and interests, or certain kinds of delinquency, or political and trade union activities; the possibility of tautology is always latent.

If 'class' is defined very narrowly, it is a concept such that simple correlations between it and other variables are purely demographic, and can be little more than starting points in the construction of complete sociological explanations; one needs to show what it is about belonging to a class that has such consequences. As Michael Young points out, it is not immediately obvious why coming from a home with a father in a certain kind of occupation should make such a difference to a child's performance in school.[46] Questions about what lies behind such correlations can only be answered by bringing in other variables, which either play an intervening role in the causal chain, or show that the correlation with class is a spurious one (i.e. that the effect is produced by something else which just happens to be associated with class).[47] Many of the kinds of explanation which a broad conception of class makes tautologous would under a narrower conception become spurious — thus, for example, if anything on closer examination could be attributed to income rather than to class *per se* the correlation between it and class would be regarded as spurious.

This may initially seem a trivial sort of distinction to make, but it has great practical as well as theoretical importance. Firstly, it is only if one starts from the narrowest sort of definition that the generalisations about patterns of empirical correlation between variables can be built up that enable the broader sort of definition to be used with some confidence that it is justified. Secondly, to the extent that the variables entering into a broad definition are less than perfectly correlated, and are capable of having some indepen-

124

dent effects, accurate predictions can only be made by treating them individually.[48] Until this is done, any deviations from a typical class pattern will remain inexplicable, and conformity will be explained only probabilistically since the mechanisms which determine it in the majority of cases will not be understood. Thus a narrower definition seems inherently preferable when, as is this case, the relationships among the variables are not already clearly known. The Institute have tended to have the worst of both worlds by using a narrow (but vague) operational definition for a broad theoretical conception.

Their use of a broad definition of class is also related to another issue, although this is not formulated as such: how far can a class be regarded as a distinct subculture? There is an ambiguity which lies at the root of many discussions of the working class: is it to be regarded as an independent entity, or as a group characterised by its place in a total class society? Any discussion in terms of subcultures, with the implied emphasis on values which lead people to *choose* to be as they are and on intergenerational continuity, tends towards the first conception; any discussion which refers its characteristics to external causes tends towards the second conception.

As Charles Valentine has pointed out in his discussion of the idea of a culture of poverty,[49] the concept of 'culture' implies that a group's way of life has its own internal logic, and that it cannot appropriately be described simply by comparison with the standards of some other group; this internal logic may not be evident from behaviour alone, which may be constrained by lack of resources. In relation to policy, the (sub)cultural conception suggests to those sympathetic towards the working class that its subculture should be supported against pressure for change and indeed encouraged to become more influential in other parts of society. (To those unsympathetic, it suggests that economic and educational disadvantages are their own fault.) The structural conception, on the other hand, suggests to them that the causes of its (superficially subcultural) traits should be eliminated by radical change in the total class structure. Thus there is potentially a moral dilemma in which sympathy towards the working class as it currently is may lead to the

125

advocacy of policies which perpetuate the effects of its structural disadvantages.

The descriptions of working-class values which run through the books of Young and Willmott* are ambiguous with respect to this issue. One gets the impression that some aspects of the total configuration of working-classness are thought of as less central than others, as more liable to change over time and less part of the basic definition of being working-class; thus, for instance, family patterns and communal solidarity seem central, but tastes in decorations, attitudes to education and length of time-perspective seem more contingent and peripheral. What makes the latter seem more peripheral is that they are treated as more the product of external factors which are regarded as *constraints* rather than simply as causes; a distinction which has strong elements of a value judgement, and which I may attribute to them unfairly.

What does not seem doubtful is that they conceive of working-class values both as having a certain autonomy and as a reaction to the place of the working class in society. The apparent contradiction is resolved by seeing the reaction as having taken place at some undefined period since the Industrial Revolution, and the autonomy and intergenerational transmission as subsequent to this origin. But there is something odd about this resolution, since if values could be formed by circumstances at one point why not at another? (They do not maintain that working-class circumstances have remained essentially unchanged, although on Marxian grounds this could be argued.) The extent to which values are shared could be attributed to similarity of structural circumstances just as well as to subcultural transmission. Frequent hints are given that changes are taking place, and that there may be differences within the working class at the present day, but it is not clear whether these phenomena are interpreted as showing that the nature of the working class is changing or merely that certain groups are leaving the working class.

Our interpretation cannot be carried beyond such a state-

* Only their books are referred to here because the others in the series do not make theoretical statements about class, though it sometimes appears as a variable.

ment of alternatives, for our authors have not formalised their positions enough for it to be evident which one they prefer, or indeed whether they are conscious of this as an issue. In this whole area of the use of 'class' greater theoretical clarification is necessary before precise explanations whose empirical fit and theoretical adequacy may be discussed seriously can be developed.

Use of Existing Theories

So much for their own theorising; we turn now to consider, much more briefly, the use made of other writers' theoretical ideas. Large numbers of references appear in the books' bibliographies, but many of these are of course not to theoretically oriented works. We may get some crude indication of their potentialities in this direction by a rough count, which reveals that the proportions of references which are to sociological or anthropological sources varies from around 12 per cent ('Patients and their Doctors') to around 67 per cent ('Widows and their Families' and 'Adolescent Boys of East London'); these are percentages of total numbers that range from 21 ('Widows and their Families') to 150 ('Innovation and Research in Education'). But such a count does not tell us anything about the manner in which the references are used, and for this we must be much more impressionistic. My own impression is that references to work with theoretical implications are usually brought towards the end of the books, as confirmation for the picture painted, rather than towards the beginning to aid in the construction of hypotheses to be tested;* this suggests that their role is not conceived as that of relating the Institute's work to the collective and cumulative enterprise of theoretical sociology. Moreover the confirmation appealed to is commonly descriptive rather than theoretical, as when, for instance, other researchers' findings about the role of Mum in working-class areas are quoted in 'Family and Kinship in East London'.

There is also a slightly different use of others' ideas, where

* Most of the books do not start in this way in any case; to that extent this obviously follows automatically.

127

they are applied *ad hoc* to suggest reasons why particular aspects of the findings should be so — as when, for instance, Ann Cartwright adduces the distinction made by Parsons et al. between instrumental and expressive roles to help explain differences between men and women in their attitudes to doctors and medicine.[50] This is a legitimate and desirable sort of use, but unless the data in hand fortuitously provide a suitable test it only gives an untested hypothesis unless the testing has already been done by the originator of the idea. (It is of course possible for new data accidentally to provide a test of an existing hypothesis, but I cannot recall any examples of this, other than the one in the next paragraph, in the oeuvre.)

The chief example of a relatively extended use of others' theoretical ideas comes in the chapter on delinquency in 'Adolescent Boys of East London'. Here the picture of the character and distribution of adolescent delinquency gained from interviews is related to mainly American theorising about the causes of juvenile (gang) delinquency, and it is concluded that the behaviour of the more seriously delinquent boys in Bethnal Green fits the predictions of the theory (pp. 160-1). But 'the' theory is in fact a large body of work within which there are considerable differences of opinion and emphasis; these cannot be glossed over by giving, as Willmott does, a sort of highest common factor account of the whole lot.

If one is concerned to see how the data fit, the theory needs to be stated more precisely. In Merton's original version, it accounted for higher crime rates among the stable working class by the society-wide prevalence of goals of material success which most of the working class could not achieve by legitimate means; this sharing of norms about desirable goals was regarded as distinctively American, while more stratified European societies were seen as having correspondingly stratified norms which kept working-class levels of aspiration low. Criminal behaviour arose from the attempt to attain shared goals by illegitimate means. For this theory to be applied to British society some modification is obviously necessary; Willmott ignores this difficulty by describing it only as involving 'the values of a prosperous and democratic society'. (In fact the great bulk of research on aspirations

128

shows that they are stratified in both Britain and America. But even for those with low aspirations the discrepancy between aspiration and opportunity may still be great; this obviously makes the argument more complicated.) The next point to note is that the theory appears to apply to the working class as a whole, but the working class as a whole is not criminal; much of the more detailed American literature suggests explanations for this. Willmott suggests that in his data it is the boys with worse school records and poorer jobs who become more seriously delinquent, but to explain why not all of these do so can only bring in (unspecified) psychological reasons; he has also somewhat confused the issue by earlier references (p. 154) to the commonness of 'white-collar crime', which imply that the phenomenon may not be even distinctively working-class as opposed to middle-class. Cloward and Ohlin[52] argued that just as legitimate opportunities are needed for respectable material success, illegitimate opportunities are needed for criminal success, and this may account for differentials among those with poor conventional opportunities; Willmott does not even refer to this possibility. A lot of the American discussion has also revolved around the question of whether there actually is a delinquent *subculture* with values that differ in crucial respects from those of respectable society; if there were, such values could be actively hostile to them (a 'contra-culture') or merely different. Considerable research, with complex results, has been done into the precise nature of the values of relevant groups.[52] Willmott does not indicate which of the different sets of conclusions he thinks his data fit, nor indeed does he describe the values of his delinquents precisely enough for the reader to make a comparison.

Finally, the argument Willmott offers for fit between data and theory is that the expressed motives and behaviour patterns of his serious delinquents correspond to those which 'the' subcultural theory would predict. This is a necessary condition for confirmation, but by no means a sufficient one; it does not indicate that the processes which the theory argues bring about this result have actually taken place, nor does it tell us that the data are not equally consistent with other theories. For the first, data on the sequence of events over time would be needed, in order to demonstrate, for

129

instance, that propensities to crime were not present *before* the experiences of failure, which might have been effect rather than cause. For the second, the alternative theories would need to be outlined and the data be such that it would be possible to discriminate among them. Neither of these conditions are met. Thus the treatment of the theoretical issues involved here is so superficial that the utility of raising them at all is very doubtful.

But this does not mean that it is not valuable, as a matter of general policy, to raise theoretical issues; quite the reverse. There are many points at which, without radical changes in the structure of the books, ideas of a general theoretical kind could profitably have been introduced into the Institute's work; some examples follow. Reference group theory[53] has a bearing on many of the issues that the Institute has been interested in; it can throw some light, for instance, on the sources of educational aspirations, on the processes involved in social mobility, and on the ways in which adolescents get drawn into one group rather than another. It could also have been relevant on some more specific points: it seems likely that doctors who felt that a high proportion of consultations were for trivial complaints[54] were less oriented to general practitioners or those with psychiatric interests as a reference group; Ann Cartwright herself suggests that some class differences in comments on hospital care may be due to the differing general expectations and experiences which the classes bring to the hospital;[55] Peter Willmott is implicitly using a reference group idea when he says that boys' attitudes to their jobs were partly determined by what they thought it was reasonable to expect from them.[56] On other topics, such sociological theorising on socialisation as Kohn's[57] and the tradition to which it belongs is obviously relevant to questions about the origins and persistence of subcultural values; the large body of theory about formal organisations, and particularly their status systems and patterns of communication, has a lot to say that can help to illuminate the modes of operation and relationship to their clients of hospitals and schools and social service organisations.[58] The purpose of bringing in these ideas would be twofold: primarily, to use the insights won in other contexts to develop greater understanding of the phenomena under study, and secondarily, to contribute in turn to the growth of theory by providing examples that help to define its scope and limits or to make needed modifications.

Conclusions

It was stated at the beginning of this chapter that the bulk of the Institute's work has been primarily descriptive in intention, with a strong orientation towards policy. We propose now to consider briefly the value, both to sociology in general and to the formulation of policy, of descriptive work. It is argued above that a more theoretical approach would have had something to offer, but this could be just an indication of scope for minor improvement rather than a positive criticism. Is the choice of approach really only a matter of taste?

The reply to this rhetorical question is, of course, yes and no. The distinction between descriptive and explanatory research is more one of degree than of kind. But once a *purpose* has been specified, the answer is much more likely to be no; only if the research is undertaken as an end in itself, with no ulterior purpose such as the advancement of sociology or the solving of social problems, can it be unequivocally yes.

This is because any description must be selective if it is not to be infinitely long; it is much more likely to be useful to anyone who wants it for a purpose if that purpose has guided the selection of aspects to be described. There are few purposes that do not entail an interest in generalising in some way from past beliefs and actions to future ones, or from the people actually studied to others. Such generalisation can only be justified by a theory about *why* the people studied should currently or in the past have their observed characteristics. If a clear theory has not yet developed, it is still more useful to try to collect data in such a way that they bear directly on potential theories than to collect it at random. The population (of events, people) to which generalisability is wanted must affect the nature of the sample studied; such relatively complex phenomena as structural

131

F

effects[59] could never be observed if the right data were not available and analysed in such a way as to bring them out, and this is unlikely to occur until the theoretical idea has been formulated. If the purpose of the research is to help form policy, which by definition entails generalising to the future, some element of theory is essential; without explanation there can be no rational prediction, only extrapolation.

But the simple inclusion of explanations is not enough their validity must also be tested. This can only be done if they are clearly stated, so that it is evident what kinds of data will count as a refutation and what as a confirmation. The Institute have rarely met this criterion. When their books start with a hypothesis to investigate it often turns out to be a popular descriptive (mis)conception — that the family no longer plays an important part in people's lives, that the inhabitants of suburbs suffer from status anxieties — which is not put precisely enough to call plainly for refutation at a level more careful than that of the original vague conception. It is useful to refute popular misconceptions by an appeal to relatively systematic data, but this is not enough for social science.

Thus our general conclusion on the theoretical side of the Institute's work must be that it has been inadequate in a variety of ways, whether judged by its contribution to sociology or by its relevance to policy-making. This does not mean that it is theoretically valueless, for it contains numbers of suggestive insights; it does mean that at least in principle the same resources could have been used more economically and to better effect. The dominant interest in policy seems to have led to an approach that aims simply to describe in order to draw practical conclusions, and defines the practical problems in such a way that others' work seems only peripherally relevant; then when the stage of analysis is reached its relevance is plain, but this is too late for its ideas to be incorporated into the design, and anyway they tend to get watered down for easy communication to the layman at whom the books are aimed. Where explanations are attempted they have a tendency to be tautological, and are usually tested weakly or not at all; this can be attributed in part to a lack of clarity and precision in the way in which they are initially stated. Whether they would, when more

132

carefully put, stand up to tests remains to be seen. Meanwhile, one aspect of the lack of clarity is a frequent absence of detail of the processes which are supposed to lead from cause to effect.

It is not obvious to the reader whether or not the superficially functionalist explanations put forward for some phenomena are really meant to express a generally functionalist standpoint; their absence in relation to other phenomena suggests not. (My guess would be that their occasional presence is due to a rather misguided desire to apply an anthropological approach worked out for small, whole and apparently static societies on which no historical data are available to parts of large societies with known histories of change. Another possibility is that they were simply forced back on this style of explanation by the absence, in the data they had collected, of anything systematic on norms, meanings or other intervening variables.) If they are not, the type of explanation really intended needs to be more carefully indicated. Functionalism has been stated explicitly as a general theoretical position, and so where passing references to it are made the informed reader can fill in the gaps for himself at that level. But for other less formalised basic positions, and for the structure of functionalist explanations of particular phenomena, more detail is needed. Until this work of explication has been done, adequacy, both 'causal' and 'on the level of meaning', is missing. For causal adequacy, a statement of the general theoretical principles from which particular findings can be seen to follow is required; for adequacy on the level of meaning, the intervening variables and motivations and perceptions of the actors involved that make the relationship between cause and effect not merely empirically given but also understandable are required.

6 Conclusions

In conclusion we shall attempt a broader and more subjective placing of the work of the Institute in its social and intellectual context; this will involve both trying to account for its special characteristics, and evaluating its total contribution to the social sciences.

The chief distinguishing characteristics of the Institute's work so far have been its descriptive approach, by means of survey research, to questions of social policy, particularly those involving the family; underlying this have been explicit or implicit value judgements about the working class and the consumers of the social services. The data collected have typically been presented in a colourful anecdotal style aimed at an audience wider than professional sociologists, and have often been drawn from a Bethnal Green sample. Not all these characteristics are, of course, entirely original, nor do all of them appear equally in all the books, but the combination gives a highly distinctive flavour.

We have argued in earlier chapters that some aspects of this combination have unfortunate consequences: that limited area samples are a poor basis for general conclusions, even in connection with policy measures; that survey method is often inappropriate for the uses to which it is put, or as employed leaves considerable scope for technical improvement; that theory as well as description is necessary for predictions on which policy can rationally be based. Can we explain why such strategies have, nonetheless, been adopted? Obviously they have been adopted because the authors have made deliberate intellectual decisions to do so, but we may still reasonably consider why they should have made one set of possible decisions rather than another.

The original choice to work in Bethnal Green need not have implied using Bethnal Green samples for so many of the studies, even though they were inspired by the earlier

134

findings; nor need the desire to compare Bethnal Green with other areas have led to further 'community' samples; but in both cases it did. It seems likely that the effort to draw on the strengths of anthropological method had something to do with both choices. Firstly, as Mitchell suggests, 'It is perhaps not without significance that this was a study of East London families, for the suggestion that they were considered among the more primitive of their English kind is hard to escape.'[1] Secondly, anthropologists have traditionally been concerned with small whole communities, treated as more or less self-sufficient units, and assumed to be closely enough integrated for their internal differentiation to be relatively unimportant. (It has long been recognised that these assumptions may not be justified, whatever their heuristic value, and that this is particularly so for small communities forming part of large complex societies.) In addition to these possible reasons it seems likely that ideas of economising research resources had something to do with the matter, and, maybe more importantly, that the authors had developed a personal intellectual commitment to this mode of research, and had become morally and socially involved in the culture of Bethnal Green in ways which transcended the making of purely rational research decisions.

The consistent use of survey techniques seems to rest on an old-fashioned conception of the survey method as inherently connected with attempts to diagnose and solve social problems, rather than as a technique of data-collection whose proper scope is not in this way definable by subject matter. This conception is nicely illustrated by Mark Abrams's well-known book, where he says:

> ... Occasionally surveys originate in an abstract desire for more knowledge about the structure and workings of society; more frequently, however, they are carried out as an indispensable first step in measuring the dimensions of a social problem, ascertaining its causes, and then deciding upon remedial action. . . .[2]

This is the familiar British tradition of Booth and Rowntree, who are acknowledged by the Institute as among their intellectual ancestors. This tradition has been primarily

135

concerned with finding out 'facts', of a broadly demographic nature, on such matters as incomes, family sizes and housing conditions, and the basic method, when applied to suitable samples and to subjects where those interviewed have little reason for concealment, is very useful for such purposes. It is less useful where individuals' behaviour rather than their 'factual' attributes is to be studied, or where for any reason (ignorance, poor memory, a desire to conceal) they are not likely to be accurate informants; it needs considerable modification if the research focuses on social relations rather than isolated individuals, or on beliefs and meanings rather than 'facts'. And, of course, neither it nor any other research technique can in itself demonstrate that a state of affairs constitutes a social problem, or suggest a solution to it if it does.

This particular historical tradition may go some way to account for the Institute's lack of concern with formal operational definitions, and the typical scarcity in their interview schedules of questions eliciting attitudes and opinions; each is relatively superfluous where the object of interest is to collect facts about simple attributes of individuals. Yet it seems at first odd that another major source in the development of modern survey technique, that of public opinion research, should not have modified this tradition's influence. But public opinion research has been much more important in America, and the Institute has always seemed surprisingly insulated from American ideas. This in turn may in part be explained by their interest in social reform, since British problems are not the same as those of America or of any other country, and so the orientation to specific problems is likely to make the experience of other countries seem less relevant. The absence of formal university affiliations may also have affected this. In a university it is more likely than in a small independent institute concentrating on applied research that new methods and ideas will be discussed for their intrinsic qualities, irrespective of any immediate use, and that contact with colleagues with diverse interests will prevent inbreeding.

The Institute's books have always been marked by a sustained effort to make their research results accessible to the broadest possible public, and one feels that this is done

136

on principle, as a matter of democracy towards potential consumers of research, as well as instrumentally to increase the chances of affecting policy. Whatever the motives, the aim is in itself an entirely laudable one. It gives rise, however, to the inevitable problem of drawing the line between popularisation and vulgarisation, between decisions about the presentation of completed research and about the way in which the research itself is done.

The distinction is an easy one to draw in principle, but often hard for the reader without inside information to make in practice. In earlier chapters we repeatedly found that the existence of evidence adequate to support the conclusions drawn was not established, and that theoretical points were not made sufficiently precisely for their import to be clear. The ordinary reader cannot know whether the researchers did really have fuller evidence for their conclusions, or whether the theoretical positions had been thought through carefully; thus he cannot tell whether the apparent weaknesses are basic ones, or just a matter of the style of presentation. Whichever is the case, the desire to popularise seems to have contributed to the effect. Anecdotes and unelaborated ideas are more easily accessible to the lay reader than tables of figures and formal hypotheses, but such accessibility may be achieved at the cost of much of the value of more rigorous research. Anecdotes can illustrate a generalisation, but not ground it; ideas elliptically thrown out can be suggestive, but not tested. When faced with the choice, the Institute has sometimes preferred accessibility to rigour, and has compounded the offence by conveying at least a superficial impression of adherence to rigorous standards which may mislead the casual reader.

But is the choice between the two styles a necessary one, or can they be reconciled? I would suggest that under many circumstances the choice need not be made. There are at least two basic kinds of solution to the problem, one of which can be adopted at a very early stage in the research and the other of which comes much later. The latter is the simpler; it consists merely of segregating the more esoteric parts of the material when the stage of writing it up for publication is reached. The most extreme way of doing this is to publish them separately as articles in learned journals, and the mildest way is to provide easy summaries in the main text of a book. Somewhere in between comes the common practice of putting supporting tables and technical details in appendices; this has often been followed by the Institute, but not usually sufficiently thoroughly to meet the criticism.

The other possible solution is not to undertake the kind of work that raises these problems, in particular not to use study designs whose logic requires detailed quantitative evidence. This is perfectly compatible with doing very respectable sociology, as work by Goffman, Becker and Gans[3] may illustrate. Their books are very readable, despite presenting unfamiliar data and interpreting it within a framework of theoretical ideas. None of them, however, attempts to convey the impression that their conclusions are based on systematic quantitative data; each author has deliberately set out to use his own sensitivities and relationships as his research instrument, and presents the findings conscious of the reservations that this may entail. Gans's book, although based on participant observation, has a subject in many ways similar to that of 'Family and Kinship in East London'; its treatment of the subject is superior as sociology partly because of the author's more theoretical orientation, and partly because he has accepted his genre and the reader knows the sources of his data and their limitations.

In the case of the Institute the creditable effort to achieve a mixture of genres and of purposes, each of which has validity on its own terms, has tended to produce a hybrid not fully satisfactory on any. Impressionistic or journalistic accounts of social problems have a valuable role to play, especially when they are based on some knowledge of social research, but they do not constitute adequate research reports; non-quantitative research methods relying on the researchers' sensitivity and insight are indispensable for many legitimate purposes, but cannot be applied to estimate the rates or incidence of facts in a population; closely documented quantitative data are for many purposes indispensable, but not likely to be persuasive, or even comprehensible, to those unfamiliar with the genre, though they may be essential to represent the full complexity of reality.

One may guess, however, that deliberate decisions about priorities do not give the whole explanation for the formal

138

looseness of presentation. The authors are not striving after 'pure' social science, and it seems probable that their moral and political value commitments have caused them both to attach less importance to rigour as a value in itself, and to be satisfied with rather low standards of proof in research whose prime object was to influence opinion. This is a serious imputation, and not one which can be made without many exceptions and reservations, but it does seem justified in some instances.

The concentration on Bethnal Green goes with this general value-orientation, for it cannot be justified on social-scientific grounds; the value of detailed knowledge of one area is far outweighed by the limitations of its unrepresentative character. But it has important emotional meanings, which are transmitted to the reader: it is a sort of Utopia, a working-class pastoral whose simple virtues show up the coldness, falsity and inhumanity of the rest of (middle-class) society. Yet it is a Utopia to be preserved rather than to be imitated; the social distance that Empson talks of as an essential part of pastoral as a mode is maintained, but the psychic satisfactions of semi-identification are no less available — perhaps even more so. As he says of the classic form of pastoral,

... The effect was in some degree to combine in the reader or author the merits of the two sorts [of people]; he was made to mirror in himself more completely the effective elements of the society he lived in.[4]

It is not surprising that such an idyllic version of (some aspect of) Bethnal Green should tend to lead to the proposal of relatively conservative solutions to its perceived problems, or that this conservatism should run into the customary difficulty of requiring some intervention in the processes that might otherwise have produced changes.

But to say all this is not to imply that the focus on Bethnal Green cannot nonetheless be justified by bringing in rather different criteria. It is not simply a Utopia, but a *counter-*Utopia, one whose function is to present an alternative. Exaggeration and idealisation can be entirely appropriate to this function, since their purpose is to emphasise those respects which are valued, and in which the Utopia differs from other

139

communities, in order to make the point about its potential advantages. The alternative implicitly under attack is the technocratic, managerial one in which planners manipulate consumers in the interest of 'efficiency' in ways which they judge to be 'for their own good', whatever the preferences of the consumers themselves may be. Bethnal Green also, of course, provides an alternative way of life to one believed to exist fairly widely in which the dominant theme is the competitive acquisition of possessions and status, and human relationships and social responsibility fall by the wayside.

It is no coincidence that the Institute started up in the middle 1950s, in the period when the postwar Labour government had left office and 'you never had it so good' became a catch phrase, and when the New Left was developing from disillusion both with Communist parties and with the effectiveness of Labour's social reforms. Key books in the movement of ideas taking place over that decade were Hoggart's 'The Uses of Literacy', Williams's 'Culture and Society' and Titmuss's 'Essays on the Welfare State',[5] all published in the late fifties when the journals 'New Left Review' and 'The New Reasoner' also started. Despite the differences of scope, subject and emphasis all these stood in one way or another for a favourable evaluation of the meanings of working-class culture, and an interpretation of it to the educated middle class; many of the writers had themselves made the transition from one to the other. This was closely linked with a movement in social administration, in which Titmuss was the leading figure, which stressed the gaps and inadequacies in welfare services, the extent to which they still left working-class material standards below those which the middle classes could take for granted, and that public policy rather than individual competence was responsible for these differences. A theme linking these two areas was the realisation that working-class people had characteristics that were not explicable simply in terms of their financial positions, so that proposals for change needed to be grounded in subtler and more complex theories. There was an intellectual euphoria in the air, with the discovery or rediscovery of the connections among politics, literature and social research. Raymond Williams's work on literature shaded over into social history and sociology, Titmuss
140

and his colleagues were directly involved in advising the Labour Party on its policies. The earlier work of the Institute, social science with a literary style and a policy orientation, fits naturally into this context of ideas and of politics, and indeed formed an intrinsic part of it, influencing as much as it was influenced.

As happens in all such movements of thought, the euphoria has died down, but this does not mean that it has been ineffectual. Many of its ideas have entered the repertoire of the conventional wisdom, even if they are still only in limited ways put into practice, and many of the leading figures now hold distinguished positions in their fields where they can influence affairs directly. The movement has become institutionalised, and the sense of excitement among the young has shifted to other causes. The Institute of Community Studies has continued and become solidly established, while its publications have tended to become more technical and less popular in their appeal, though still holding to the same ethos and tradition.

Perhaps it is too soon to talk about the historical role of the Institute in British sociology, but a few words must be said about this. Many people would argue that it had an inspiring and vivifying effect on a situation where respectable social research was rare, and sociology as an academic subject was only taught in a few universities. It is hard to estimate such an effect without some detailed research into intellectual history, which has yet to be undertaken. Various pieces of research on subjects related to those studied by the Institute had been published or were under way by the middle of the 1950s — for example, Mogey's 'Family and Neighbourhood', Glass et al.'s 'Social Mobility in Britain', Spinley's 'The Deprived and the Privileged', Bott's 'Family and Social Network', Dennis et al.'s 'Coal is our Life', Floud et al.'s 'Social Class and Educational Opportunity'.[6] This list could be extended, though certainly not by a large number of significant titles. None of these others seems to have caught the public imagination in the same way as 'Family and Kinship in East London', though many of them could claim to be better as social science.

My own impression is that the influence of the Institute's work within the social sciences strictly defined has been small, although it is regularly used; that is, the work is acceptable as data, with greater or lesser reservations, but has not made a substantial difference to the pattern of work done by other people. Its major sphere of influence has been outside the social sciences, among planners and social workers and more generally on educated public opinion; this may well be as the authors would prefer, and thus an index of their success in achieving their objects. But I think that it has had one significant indirect consequence for sociology, in arousing the interest of young people who are potential recruits to the field; I number myself among the generation for whom their work, with that of David Riesman,[7] went to create an atmosphere of excitement about sociology which altered the pattern of many careers. Those of us who have stayed in the field do not necessarily end up doing work that resembles the Institute's, but the influence has not been the less significant for that. If the Institute's historical role had been to generate more research of the same character as its own, this might have been unfortunate, for, as we have shown, its example is not an altogether desirable one for sociologists. If, however, it has produced a generalised enthusiasm for social research rather than direct imitation it has played a very valuable role.

The character of its influence must not be judged by its own character but by the meanings this has had for other people, and these may be highly selective. One possibility has been mentioned; another is that it has contributed to the fairly prevalent ideas that sociology is always about problems of social welfare, and that the survey technique is its sole and defining method of data collection. To the extent that this is so it has done sociology a disservice, but not a very important one so long as the ideas are confined to non-sociologists. (It is a pity that the earliest books remain those by which most people know the Institute.)

Some of these judgements may appear parochial to sociology, and indeed to one particular conception of sociology, but they do not rest simply on differences in intellectual taste — though these are present. Books can be written that are effective both as empirical sociology and as support for a social pressure group, that are concerned with theoretical problems as well as with social ones; where claims are made to attempt both, the results must be judged by the

142

criteria appropriate to both.

Our total evaluation of the work of the Institute of Community Studies as a whole, then, must be one which rates its contribution to thought about planning and social welfare and to effective political pressure very highly, but which regards its direct contribution to sociology with considerable reservations. There is every reason to believe that it will continue to perform useful functions, and that the encouraging recent signs of a break with some aspects of its tradition may lead to further improvements in the weaker aspects of its research. It is hoped that this critical review may help in the establishment of a balanced perspective on its role in British sociology and social research.

Notes

1 *Introduction*

1. Michael Young and Peter Willmott, 'Research Report No. 3: Institute of Community Studies, Bethnal Green', in 'Sociological Review', ix (July 1961) 203-13.
2. Information provided by the Institute.
3. 'Times Literary Supplement', 16 Dec 1960, p. 815.
4. 'Daily Telegraph', 9 Mar 1963.
5. 'The Economist', 2 Dec 1961, p. 898.
6. 'Sociological Review', xi (July 1963) 256.
7. 'Sunday Times', 10 Mar 1963, p. 29.
8. 'American Sociological Review', xxix 1 (Feb 1964) 152.
9. Ibid., xxxiii 6 (Dec 1968) 997-8.
10. In particular in two books summarising large bodies of research: Josephine Klein, 'Samples from English Cultures' (Routledge & Kegan Paul, 1965); Ronald Frankenberg, 'Communities in Britain' (Penguin, 1966). They are also frequently mentioned in footnotes to work on various aspects of family relationships in industrial societies and the bearing on them of class differences.
11. Colin Rosser and Christopher Harris, 'The Family and Social Change: A Study of Family and Kinship in a South Wales Town' (Routledge & Kegan Paul, 1965).
12. I.e. Brian Jackson, Dennis Marsden and W. G. Runciman.

2 *Value Judgements and Policy Recommendations*

1. See Ch. 1, Introduction pp. 1-2.
2. (27) p. 139.
3. (23) p. 5.
4. (17) p. 107.
5. (18) p. 134.

6. (8) p. 110.
7. E.g. in (1) p. 161.
8. See pp. 76-7, 96-7, 118-20.
9. (48) p. 770.
10. (13) pp. 176-7.
11. (12) pp. 71 and 82.
12. (46) p. 48.
13. See Elizabeth Bott, 'Family and Social Network' (Tavistock, 1957) chs iii and iv.
14. 'The People of Ship Street' (Routledge & Kegan Paul, 1958) pp. 8-9.
15. 'British Journal of Sociology', xvii 1 (1966) 79.
16. 'The Rise of the Meritocracy' (Thames & Hudson, 1958).
17. For a theoretical discussion of the range of possibilities, see A. Gouldner, 'Reciprocity and Autonomy in Functional Theory', in 'Symposium on Sociological Theory', ed. L. Gross (Harper & Row, New York, 1959).
18. (16) ch. viii.
19. For a discussion of ways in which this may happen, see Jennifer Platt, 'Some Problems in Measuring the Jointness of Conjugal Role-Relationships', in 'Sociology', iii 3 (Sept 1969) 287-97.
20. See p. 78.
21. S. T. Bruyn, 'The Human Perspective in Sociology' (Prentice-Hall, Englewood Cliffs, N.J., 1966) p. 250.
22. Richard Hoggart, 'The Uses of Literacy' (Penguin, 1958) pp. 53-4.

3 Research Methods: The Old Tradition

1. (2) ch. ix.
2. The other two possible answers are 'can't say' and 'refuse'.
3. For a brief discussion and references, see John H. Goldthorpe and David Lockwood, 'Affluence and the British Class Structure', in 'Sociological Review', xi 2 (July 1963) 143-4.
4. (1) p. 72.
5. W. S. Robinson, 'Ecological Correlations and the Behaviour of Individuals', in 'American Sociological

Review', xv (1950) 351-7.
6. See, for example, Paul F. Lazarsfeld and Morris Rosenberg (eds), 'The Language of Social Research' (Free Press, Glencoe, Ill., 1955); Herbert Hyman, 'Survey Design and Analysis' (Free Press, New York, 1955).
7. Bott, 'Family and Social Network', ch. iv.
8. Mark Lefton, in 'American Sociological Review', xxix (Feb 1964) 152.
9. See pp. 55-6, 67.
10. For a discussion of related issues, see Margaret Stacey, 'The Myth of Community Studies', in 'British Journal of Sociology', xx 2 (June 1969) 134-47.
11. For a discussion of structural effects, see P. M. Blau, 'Structural Effects', in 'American Sociological Review', xxv (1960) 178-92.
12. For discussion of the use of deviant cases, see William J. Goode and Paul K. Hatt, 'Methods in Social Research' (McGraw-Hill, 1952) pp. 88-9; Lazarsfeld and Rosenberg (eds), 'The Language of Social Research', section II, C.

4 Research Methods: Newer Models

1. University Grants Committee, 'Returns from Universities and University Colleges in Receipt of Treasury Grant' (H.M.S.O.), for the academic years 1960-1 or 1961-2.
2. See, for example, Liam Hudson, 'Contrary Imaginations' (Methuen, 1966) ch. 2.
3. Full details are given in app. 1.
4. Described in ch. 4.
5. See p. 14.

5 Theory

1. Hyman, 'Survey Design and Analysis', ch. ii.
2. R. K. Merton, 'Social Theory and Social Structure', revised ed. (Free Press, Glencoe, Ill.,) chs ii and iii; David Willer, 'Scientific Sociology: Theory and Method' (Prentice-Hall, Englewood Cliffs, N.J., 1967) ch. 6.
3. Merton, 'Social Theory and Social Structure', pp. 5-10.
146

4. John Rex, 'Key Problems of Sociological Theory' (Routledge & Kegan Paul, 1961), esp. ch. ix.
5. (1) p. 71.
6. (1) pp. 157-8.
7. (1) p. 156.
8. (2) p. 79.
9. (1) p. 159.
10. (1) p. 80.
11. (4) pp. 84-5.
12. (1) ch. i.
13. (2) p. 75; see also the footnote on p. 76.
14. (4) p. 76.
15. (1) pp. 6-10.
16. (1) ch. iv.
17. For discussion of the issues, see: Merton, 'Social Theory and Social Structure', ch. i; Marion J. Levy, Jr, 'The Structure of Society' (Princeton University Press, 1952) chs i and ii; Carl G. Hempel, 'The Logic of Functional Analysis', in 'Symposium on Sociological Theory', ed. Gross.
18. (2) p. 113.
19. (5) p. 138; (46) pp. 45-9.
20. (1) p. 158.
21. See Ch. 3, 'Research Methods: The Old Tradition', pp. 53, 60.
22. (4) p. 106.
23. See Ch. 2, 'Value Judgements and Policy Recommendations', p. 21.
24. Bott, 'Family and Social Network', p. 60.
25. (2) p. 76.
26. Bott, 'Family and Social Network', pp. 92 and 78. For related comments, see J. A. Barnes, 'Graph Theory and Social Networks: a Technical Comment on Connectedness and Connectivity', in 'Sociology', iii 2 (May 1969) 215-32, esp. 225.
27. Lee Rainwater, 'Family Design' (Aldine, Chicago, 1965), esp. chs 2 and 10.
28. This description draws on a variety of sources, of which the main ones are the 'Conclusions' of 'Family and Kinship in East London' and 'Family and Class in a London Suburb', and ch. iv of 'Innovation and Research

in Education'.

29. (12) pp. 66-71.
30. (1) pp. 144-54.
31. (8) ch. v.
32. (1) pp. 141-4; (4) chs iii, iv, vii.
33. (4) p. 132.
34. (1) pp. 134-5.
35. (4) p. 128.
36. (4) pp. 129-32; see also (8) p. 100.
37. (1) pp. 127-9.
38. (4) pp. 114-16.
39. The only reference I can find to this is in 'The Evolution of a Community', p. 73, which also gives in a footnote the sources for other researchers' use of the distinction. For discussion of 'deferential' workers, see Robert McKenzie and Allan Silver, 'Angels in Marble' (Heinemann, 1968), esp. ch. 5; Eric A. Nordlinger, 'The Working Class Tories' (MacGibbon & Kee, 1967); David Lockwood, 'Sources of Variation in Working Class Images of Society', in 'Sociological Review', xiv 3 (Nov 1966) 249-67.
40. See Ch. 4, 'Research Methods: Newer Models', p. 96.
41. For an example of this problem in another context, see K. P. Johnson and G. R. Leslie, 'Methodological Notes on Research in Childrearing and Social Class', in 'Merrill Palmer Quarterly', ii 4 (Oct 1965).
42. (46) p. 45; (48) p. 768.
43. See Ch. 3, 'Research Methods: The Old Tradition', p. 62.
44. (4) p. 160; for further discussion of this procedure, see Ch. 3, p. 61.
45. (1) p. 72.
46. (12) p. 61.
47. For an extended example of the way in which this can be done, see Ch. 3, 'Research Methods: The Old Tradition', p. 63.
48. For an example of a quite different case where the variables specified in a broad definition are not in practice sufficiently correlated, see Stanley H. Udy, Jr, 'Bureaucracy' and 'Rationality' in Weber's Organization Theory: an Empirical Study', in 'American Sociological Review', xxiv 6 (Dec

1959) 791-5.
49. Charles Valentine, 'Culture and Poverty' (University of Chicago Press, 1969) p. 12.
50. (15) p. 195.
51. Richard A. Cloward and Lloyd E. Ohlin, 'Delinquency and Opportunity' (Routledge & Kegan Paul, 1961) ch. 7.
52. See, for example, J. Milton Yinger, 'Contraculture and Subculture', in 'American Sociological Review', xxv 5 (Oct 1960) 625-35; David Matza and Gresham M. Sykes, 'Juvenile Delinquency and Subterranean Values', in 'American Sociological Review', xxvi 5 (Oct 1961) 712-19; Robert A. Gordon et al., 'Values and Gang Delinquency . . .', in 'American Journal of Sociology', lxix 2 (Sept 1963) 109-28.
53. See Merton, 'Social Theory and Social Structure', chs viii and ix; (14) ch. ii.
54. (15) ch. iv.
55. (9) ch. xv.
56. (13) p. 111.
57. Melvin L. Kohn, 'Social Class and Parent–Child Relationships: An Interpretation', in 'American Journal of Sociology', lxvii 4 (Jan 1963) 471-80.
58. For a general text in this area, see Peter M. Blau and W. Richard Scott, 'Formal Organisations' (Routledge & Kegan Paul, 1963).
59. See Ch. 4, 'Research Methods: Newer Models', p. 96.

6 *Conclusions*

1. G. Duncan Mitchell, 'A Hundred Years of Sociology' (Duckworth, 1968) p. 263.
2. Mark Abrams, 'Social Surveys and Social Action' (Heinemann, 1951) p. 2.
3. E. Goffman, 'The Presentation of Self in Everyday Life' (Anchor Books, Doubleday, New York, 1959); Howard S. Becker, 'Outsiders' (Free Press, Glencoe, Ill., 1963); Herbert J. Gans, 'The Urban Villagers' (Free Press, Glencoe, Ill., 1962).
4. William Empson, 'Some Versions of Pastoral' (Chatto & Windus, 1935) p. 12.

5. Richard Hoggart, 'The Uses of Literacy' (Chatto & Windus, 1957); Raymond Williams, 'Culture and Society' (Chatto & Windus, 1958); Richard M. Titmuss, 'Essays on the Welfare State' (Allen & Unwin, 1958).

6. J. M. Mogey, 'Family and Neighbourhood' (Oxford University Press, 1956); D. Glass (ed.), 'Social Mobility in Britain' (Routledge & Kegan Paul, 1954); B. M. Spinley, 'The Deprived and the Privileged' (Routledge & Kegan Paul, 1953); Elizabeth Bott, 'Family and Social Network' (Tavistock, 1957); N. Dennis, F. Henriques and C. Slaughter, 'Coal Is Our Life' (Eyre & Spottiswoode, 1956); Jean Floud, A. H. Halsey and F. Oppenheimer, 'Social Class and Educational Opportunity' (Heinemann, 1957).

7. David Riesman, Nathan Glazer and Reuel Denney, 'The Lonely Crowd' (Yale University Press, 1950).

Bibliography of Works by the Institute of Community Studies

Books in the Institute of Community Studies series (all published by Routledge & Kegan Paul).

1957   1. Michael Young and Peter Willmott, 'Family and Kinship in East London'.
       2. Peter Townsend, 'The Family Life of Old People'.
1958   3. Peter Marris, 'Widows and their Families'.
1960   4. Peter Willmott and Michael Young, 'Family and Class in a London Suburb'.
1961   5. Peter Marris, 'Family and Social Change in an African City'.
1962   6. Enid Mills, 'Living with Mental Illness'.
       7. Brian Jackson and Dennis Marsden, 'Education and the Working Class'.
1963   8. Peter Willmott, 'The Evolution of a Community'.
1964   9. Ann Cartwright, 'Human Relations and Hospital Care'.
      10. Peter Marris, 'The Experience of Higher Education'.
      11. Brian Jackson, 'Streaming: An Education System in Miniature'.
1965 12. Michael Young, 'Innovation and Research in Education'.
1966 13. Peter Willmott, 'Adolescent Boys of East London'.
      14. W. G. Runciman, 'Relative Deprivation and Social Justice'.
1967 15. Ann Cartwright, 'Patients and their Doctors'.
      16. Peter Marris and Martin Rein, 'Dilemmas of Social Reform'.
1968 17. Michael Young and Patrick McGeeney, 'Learning Begins at Home'.

151

Articles, papers etc. based on work done at the Institute of Community Studies. Reprints of most of these are available in the Institute's series, but note that the numbering here differs slightly from that used there because this list excludes articles by members of the Institute's staff which are not strictly based on their research at the Institute.

1954   18. Michael Young, 'The Planners and the Planned: The Family', in 'Journal of the Town Planning Institute', xi 6 (May 1954) 134-42.

19. Michael Young, 'The Role of the Extended Family in a Disaster', in 'Human Relations', vii 3 (July 1954) 383-991.

20. Michael Young, 'Kinship and Family in East London', in 'Man', liv (Sept 1954) 137-9.

1955   21. Peter Townsend, 'The Anxieties of Retirement', in 'Transactions of the Association of Industrial Medical Officers', v 1, (Aug 1955) 19-24.

22. Peter Townsend, 'The Family Life of Old People', in 'Sociological Review', iii 2 (Dec 1955) 175-95.

1956   23. Michael Young, 'The Extended Family Welfare Association', in 'Social Work', xiii 1 (Jan 1956) 145-50.

24. Michael Young and Peter Willmott, 'Social Grading by Manual Workers', in 'British Journal of Sociology', iii (Dec 1956) 337-45.

1958   25. Peter Willmott, 'Social Administration and Social Class', in 'Case Conference', iv 7 (Jan 1958) 194-8.

26. Peter Willmott and Philip Barbour, 'Housing of Old People in a Rural Parish', in 'Social Service Quarterly', xxxi 4 (spring 1958) 158-61.

27. Peter Willmott, 'Kinship and Social Legislation', in 'British Journal of Sociology', ix 2 (June 1958) 126-42.

1960   28. Peter Marris, 'Social Change and Social Class', in 'International Journal of Comparative Sociology', i 1 (Mar 1960) 119-24.

29. Peter Marris, 'Slum Clearance and Family Life in Lagos', in 'Human Organisation', xix (autumn 1960) 123-8.

30. E. W. Cooney, 'The Leagues of Hospital Friends', in 'Public Administration', xxxviii (autumn 1960) 263-72.

1961   31. Michael Young and Hildren Geertz, 'Old Age in London and San Francisco', in 'British Journal of Sociology', xii (June 1961) 124-41.

32. Michael Young and Peter Willmott, 'The Institute of Community Studies', in 'Sociological Review', x 2 (July 1961) 203-13.

1962   33. Peter Willmott, 'Housing Density and Town Design in a New Town', in 'Town Planning Review', xxxiii (July 1962) 115-27.

34. Peter Marris, 'The Social Implications of Urban Redevelopment', in 'Journal of the American Institute of Planners', xxviii (Aug 1962) 180-6.

1963   35. Phyllis and Peter Willmott, 'Off Work through Illness', in 'New Society', i 15 (10 Jan 1963) 16-18.

36. Peter Marris, 'Urban Renewal in the United States', in 'The Urban Condition', ed. Leonard J. Duhl (Basic Books, New York) 113-34.

37. Michael Young and John Gibson, 'In Search of an Explanation of Social Mobility', in 'British Journal of Statistical Psychology', xvi (1) (May 1963) 27-36.

38. Michael Young, Bernard Benjamin and Chris Wells, 'The Mortality of Widowers', in 'The Lancet', ii (31 Aug 1963) 454-6.

39. Peter Willmott and Edmund Cooney, 'Community Planning and Sociological Research', in 'Journal of the American Institute of Planners', xxix (May 1963) 123-6.

1964   40. Peter Willmott, 'East Kilbride and Stevenage', in 'Town Planning Review', xxxiv (Jan 1964) 307-16.

41. Richard MacCormac and Peter Willmott, 'Housing at Chells, Stevenage', in 'Architect's Journal', (25 Mar 1964) 691-5.

42. Peter Willmott, 'Housing in Cumbernauld', in 'Journal of the Town Planning Institute', l (May 1964) 195-200.

1965   43. Ann Cartwright and Rosalind Marshall, 'General Practice in 1963', in 'Medical Care', iii 2 (April-June 1965) 69-87.

1967   44. Ann Cartwright and Wyn Tucker, 'An Attempt to Reduce the Number of Calls on an Interview Survey', in 'Public Opinion Quarterly', xxxi (summer 1967) 299-302.

45. Nick Reid, 'Housing in Basildon', in 'Journal of the Town Planning Institute', iii (July-Aug 1967) 297-301.

46. Peter Marris, 'Motives and Methods: Reflections on a Study in Lagos', in 'The City in Modern Africa', ed Horace Miner (Pall Mall Press) pp. 39-54.

47. Peter Willmott, 'Social Research and New Communities', in 'Journal of the American Institute of Planners', xxxiii (Nov 1967) 387-97.

48. Peter Marris, 'Individual Achievement and Family Ties: Some International Comparisons', in 'Journal of Marriage and the Family', xxix 4 (Nov 1967) 763-71.

49. Peter Marris, 'Lending Money', in 'Journal of Modern African Studies', v 2 (1967) 221-31.

1968   50. Peter Willmott, 'A Code for Research', in 'Times Literary Supplement', 4 April 1968, special supplement on sociology.

51. Ann Cartwright, 'Communication between Doctors and Patients', in 'Proceedings of the Royal Society of Medicine', lx 6 (June 1968) 561-3 (Library (Scientific Research) Section, pp. 11-13).

52. H. Houghton, 'Problems of Hospital Communication', in 'Problems and Progress in Medical Care', ed. G. MacLachlan (Oxford University Press, 1968) 115-43.

53. Ann Cartwright, 'General Practitioners and Family Planning', in 'The Medical Officer', cxx 3 (19 July 1968) 43-6.

54. Peter Marris, 'The Social Barriers in African Entrepreneurship', in 'Journal of Development Studies', v 1 (Oct 1968) 29-38.

154

1969   55. May Clarke, 'Feet: A Study of Foot Troubles and their Care', in 'Occasional Papers in Social Administration', no. 29 (Bell, 1969).

        56. Peter Willmott, 'Some Social Trends', in 'Urban Studies', vi 3 (Nov 1969) 286-308.

Since the text of this book was written, another work in the Institute of Community Studies series has been published:

1970   Ann Cartwright, 'Parents and Family Planning Services'.

Index

157

158

Intervening variables, need for, 59-60, 63-4, 123-4, 133
Interview schedules 78
   'Adolescent Boys of East London', 71-2
   'Family and Class in a London Suburb', 56-8
   'Family and Kinship in East London', 48
   'Family and Social Change in an African City', 81
   'Learning Begins at Home', 89
   'Living with Mental Illness', 68
   'Widows and their Families', 66

Jackson, Brian, 5, 144
Jointness, see Conjugal Roles
Juvenile delinquency, see Delinquency

Labour theory of value, see Working-class values
'Learning begins at Home', 87-92
   analysis, 89-90
   experimental design, 87-8
   findings, 90-1
   interview schedule, 89
   samples, 87, 91
   values, their effect on conclusions of, 91-2
'Living with Mental Illness', 67-8
   interview schedule, 68
   review of, quoted, 7-8
   sample, 68

Marris, Peter, 5-6
Marsden, Dennis, 5, 144
Methods of research, see Research methods
Middle class
   culture, 113
   differentiation of, 116
   values, 113-14
Mills, Enid, 5
Mother—daughter tie (see also Conjugal roles, Family), 102-3, 107-8
Multivariate analysis
   absence of, 59-60, 64, 70, 93
   use of, 73, 83, 86

Norms, explanatory relevance of, 106-12 passim

Occupational classification
   and style of life, 121-3
   in 'Adolescent Boys of East London', 73, 121

in 'Evolution of a Community, The', 70
in 'Family and Class in a London Suburb', 61-2
use of Registrar-General's, 120
Open-ended questions, see Coding
Operational definitions
   class, 61-2, 120-3
   house-centredness, 53
   inadequacy of, 53, 60, 78, 93
   reasons for inadequacy of, 136

'Patients and their Doctors', 84-6
   analysis, 86
   classification of patients, 85-6
   policy recommendations, 24-8
   review of, quoted, 8
   sample, 84
Policy recommendations
   conservatism of, 22-3, 33, 37, 139
   consumer viewpoint and, 34-40
   criteria for good ones, 18-19, 33
   'Family and Kinship in East London', 19-21
   'Family Life of Old People, The', 21-4
   Functional alternatives, 19-20
   'Innovation and Research in Education', 28-30
   'Patients and their Doctors', 24-8
   social costs and, 18-31 passim
   sociological theory and, 32-3
   survey data, relation to, 34-8
   values of the researcher and, 34-8
Popularisation
   and vulgarisation, the line between, 137-8
   can it be reconciled with rigour?, 66, 97, 137-8
Pressure group, Institute as, see Institute of Community Studies

Questionnaires, see Interview schedules
Quotations, use of, 49-52, 65, 68, 70, 72, 81, 83, 89, 93, 137

Reference group theory, relevance of, 130
'Relative Deprivation and Social Justice', 4, 9
Research methods
   in 'Adolescent Boys of East London', 70-5
   in 'Dilemmas of Social Reform', 87

159

160

interview schedule, 66
sample, 66-7
Willmott, Peter, 5-6
Woodford
  not compared with Greenleigh, 62
  reasons for choice of, 54
  satisfaction with, seen as compla-
    cency, 14
  treated as middle-class community,
    62
  working class in, 57-8, 117-18
Working class
  as sub-culture, 125-6

atypical aspirations in, 117-18
culture described, 112-13
culture, discovery of, in 1950s, 140
culture, explanation of, 114-16
differentiation within, 73, 117-18,
  121
in Woodford, 57-8, 117-18
Working-class values, 112-13, 126
  autonomy of, 126
  lack of evidence on prevalence of,
    119

Young, Michael, 5-6

32123331223 21

\